ENGLISH ✶ HERITA

Book of
Canals

29

ENGLISH ❖ HERITAGE

Book of
Canals

Nigel Crowe

B.T. Batsford Ltd/English Heritage
London

Typeset by Lasertext Ltd, Stretford, Manchester
and printed in Great Britain by
The Bath Press, Bath

Published by B. T. Batsford Ltd
4 Fitzhardinge Street, London W1H 0AH
A CIP catalogue record for this book is available from the British Library
ISBN 0 7134 6883 1 (cased)
0 7134 6884 x (limp)

Contents

Illustrations

Colour Plates

Between pages 64 and 65

Foreword

The inland waterways thread their way across most of Britain, linking major towns and cities with some of our loveliest countryside. They form an almost secret world which is a microcosm of special landscapes, wildlife habitats and — above all — that indefinable thing 'heritage'. And not just the obvious structures: the locks, aqueducts and tunnels, but magnificent canalside warehouses and dock buildings; tollhouses; lifting, swinging and rolling bridges; barrel-roofed lock cottages; mileposts, mooring rings and all the paraphernalia of canalside 'trim' and, of course, the remarkable painted craft of the boating communities.

The birth of the inland waterways network changed the face of the countryside for ever. Two hundred years ago, in the Canal Mania of 1793 and 1794, speculation in canal building schemes reached its zenith. In just two years, 38 Acts of Parliament were authorised. We can only imagine the impact on eighteenth-century Britain.

The Duke of Bridgewater's private enterprise ignited the spark of Canal Mania. Thereafter, canal building plans abounded on a rollercoaster of get-rich-quick speculations. No less than 62 different canals — half the entire navigable waterway system of Britain — were being worked on in 1793 alone. Within just three decades, it became possible to move large cargoes over great distances. The transport arteries of the canal system have rightly been described as carrying the lifeblood of the Industrial Revolution.

Today's still, dark ribbon of water at the back of the town, or reed-edged silver streak glimpsed across fields, identified as a canal only by the bold black and white of lock gate beams, is the same waterway that fattened the industries of the nation. Once the canal system drew the country together; today its slow course stretches a world more used to the instantly accessible.

The initial raw scar of the construction mellowed by two centuries of nature's attrition, the waterways today are highways to kingfishers and damselflies; wildlife happily coexisting with over 20,000 boats and the millions who come to soak up the atmosphere of this special and historic environment. Some 2,000 miles of inland waterways are conserved and managed for the nation by British Waterways.

Dr Nigel Crowe, British Waterways' Heritage Manager, reveals how these waterways evolved. Much of the research for his book was undertaken during the Architectural Heritage Survey, funded jointly by British Waterways and English Heritage, which began in 1988 and still continues.

This mammoth undertaking involves surveying and recording the buildings and structures along every mile of British Waterways' 2,000-mile system, from Inverness to Bath, from Llangollen to Boston: 4,763 bridges, 1,549 locks, 397 aqueducts, 60 tunnels and hundreds of canal-related buildings. The results of this task, when finally completed in the mid 1990s, will be a unique and invaluable record of the man-made environment of the inland waterways, from the simple cast-iron milestone to grand Victorian warehouses.

In Nigel Crowe's book we have a scholarly yet evocative record of the rich legacy of 'heritage' that is Britain's unique canal system today.

The Chairman
British Waterways

Preface

England's canals were the last crucial harnessing of a centuries-old heavy transport medium — water. They represent the point of collision between the pre-industrial, handmade world and the new industrial world of the machine, of processes and prefabrication. The canal network was an invented, enclosed world, where every waterway had its own flavour, its own atmosphere. Much of that atmosphere, especially the sense of enclosure, was generated by buildings; by the architecture of locks, bridges, aqueducts and tunnels, and by maintenance yards, boatyards, wharfs, warehouses and dwellings. The context was straightforward, the dialect of forms simple, the palette of materials limited. Yet local and regional differences abounded. The details, even of oft-repeated architectural forms, were varied and there was much modification, adaptation and renewal. Canal building was conditioned by landscape, function, finance, company policy or an engineer's genius. This was the great age of empirical engineering and on canals architecture and engineering blur and separate and blur again.

This is not a history of canals. It deals mainly with English canals, although there are references to Ireland, Scotland and Wales. It glances back at the origins of inland water transport in England and discusses river navigations, with which canals often intertwine or connect. But the main focus of this book is the Georgian Canal Age, that restless, energetic period when England was penetrated by waterways which fed the Industrial Revolution.

This book is about the architecture of those waterways. It describes the structures and buildings that were created, the functions they fulfilled, the way they performed and the lives which were played out in, around, or forever passing them, in that final working world constructed around the horse.

Much of the information on which this book is based has emerged from the jointly funded British Waterways/English Heritage Architectural Heritage Survey. I would like to acknowledge staff from both organizations for their assistance and support and in particular the following: Peter White (former Chief Architect at British Waterways), Peter White (RCAHM Wales), Anthony Streeten, Judy Grice, Vanessa Wiggins, Pete Smith and Martin Cherry. More specifically I wish to thank Roy Jamieson for his great help in locating material from British Waterways' archives and for permitting me to use photographs from the unique Arthur Watts Collection; Mary Murphy for showing me drawings owned by the Institution of Civil Engineers; Gary Tonks; Steve Boakes for showing me round Bull's Bridge Yard before it vanished. I owe especial thanks to Roger Butler for the use of his colour photographs. The excellent maps and reconstructions were drawn by Peter Dunn of English Heritage. Others who deserve my gratitude include R.J.M. Sutherland who gave some kind advice, Peter

Wakelin, and Frederick Bryan-Brown who read my text and offered helpful criticism, and my editors Stephen Johnson, and Charlotte Kilenyi. I want to thank Simon and Tanya Green and Alastair Marshall for going boating with me. Finally, I owe a debt to all the old canal men whom I met on my travels round England and who passed on much by way of anecdote and improbable history.

This book is dedicated to my parents, to my wife Alison who typed the whole thing out and to my son Thomas who was born as I wrote the final chapter.

1 *Map of waterways in England, Scotland and Wales mentioned in the text* (P. Dunn).

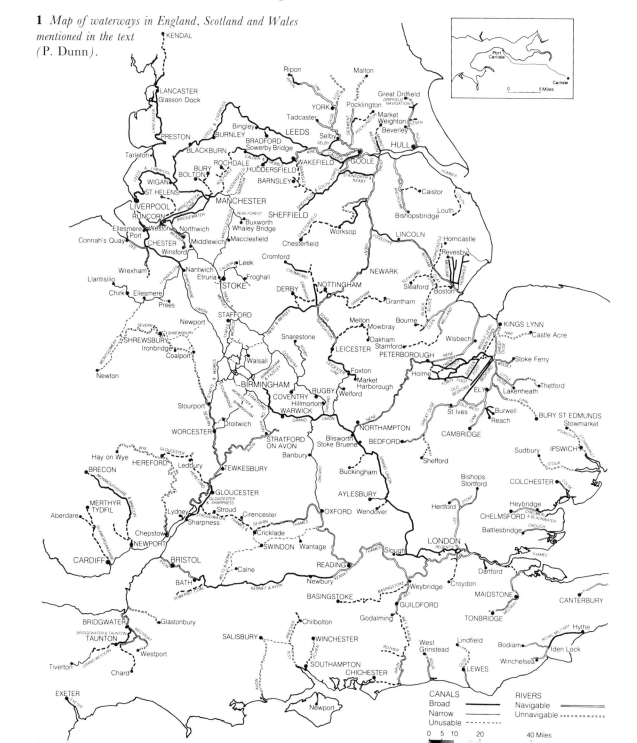

1

River navigations and canals

England is a land of ditches, streams and small rivers, the 'cherishing veines of the body of every Countrey, Kingdome, and Nation', especially of a seafaring nation whose history has much to do with fighting, travelling and trading on water. From early times England's coastal and riverside settlements developed a pattern of economic activity involving transport of goods by sea, by rivers and finally by canals.

Canals were the heavy goods routes of pre-railway England and like the first railways they were local, or at best regional, arteries of trade. They meshed with an expanding network of horse tramways, parish and turnpike roads, river navigations and ports and harbours. Canal construction required special knowledge and skill and the creation of a range of new engineering structures and buildings. But before focusing on the architectural qualities of canals we must glance back to their origins, to the organisation behind them and to the controlling background of the Industrial Revolution which created in England a canal age, with recognizable heroes, styles, and buildings of its own.

Early waterways

By the second century AD the Romans had created a well-organized transport system in England, based mainly on roads and rivers. The Romans also built canals, but their purpose is not clear. These 'canals' were constructed by skilled military engineers and soldiers; the Foss Dyke was probably navigable between Lincoln and the Trent, from where York could be reached via the Humber and Ouse. At Lincoln the Witham was 'improved' and traces of a wharf found there may be Roman. The Cambridgeshire Car Dyke and a series of minor canals or lodes linked to the Cam may be Roman in origin. Land drainage, especially in the rich fenlands, was a constant problem and was probably the main reason for these early canals. Evidence for the Roman use of navigable rivers is more reliable. The Severn, Trent,

1a *The canals of Scotland*

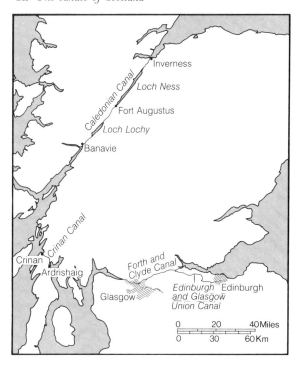

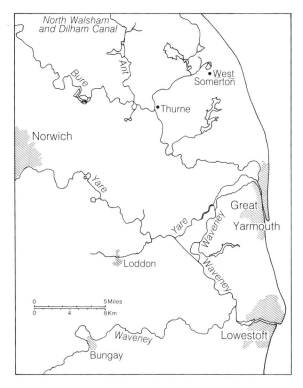

1b *The Norfolk Broads*

Throughout the Middle Ages the main river systems remained more or less navigable as local conditions and weather allowed. But rivers were sources of food and power as well as transport, and this led to a conflict of interests. Mill-owners built dams and sluices to maintain a steady supply of water to turn their wooden wheels. Bridges, fords, fisheries and embankments formed other obstacles to navigation. Town councils and bridge owners often tried to exact tolls on river carriage. Added to these were natural nuisances like shoals, shifting sand, drought and the sheer difficulty of sailing or hauling boats against the current.

Despite the hazards, the usefulness of rivers for carrying heavy goods such as coal, corn, timber and wool, was undeniable and legislation designed to keep rivers open to navigation was passed from time to time. Corpor-

1c *Canals and rivers of East London*

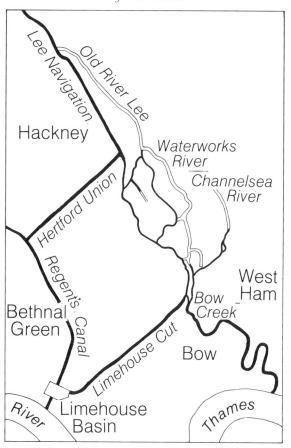

Ouse, Great Ouse, Avon, Nene and Dee had garrison towns and provincial capitals located on their banks. The Thames rapidly became England's most important commercial transport route. For the next 1500 years the key to a town's growth and prosperity was the existence of a navigable river.

The Saxons made good use of England's rivers, still tidal far inland and the most reliable means of long-distance communication in forested and sparsely inhabited country. The word 'hythe' is Old English for a small haven or landing-place on a river: probably a cluster of mud-and-timber huts, some sheds and wooden staging. Some of these hythes evolved into inland ports as populations grew and trade intensified. By the eleventh century London was well established as capital city and major port and at London's heart were the wharfs along its riverside.

England's medieval rivers flowed 'like streams in a missal' through an unspoilt land.

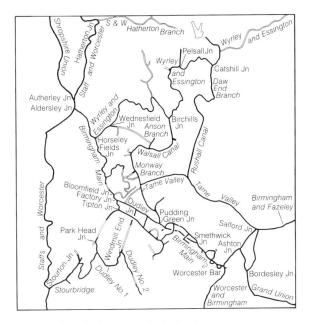

1d *The Birmingham Canal Navigations*

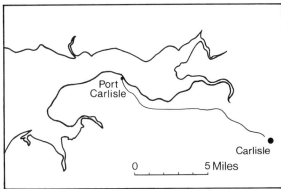

1e *Carlisle Canal*

ations and individuals were sometimes given control of certain rivers and allowed to collect tolls. In Essex the Roding was controlled by Barking Abbey. Beverley Beck was controlled by Beverley Corporation. The Archbishop of York collected tolls on the River Hull. The Thames was administered by Crown servants. And from the thirteenth century onwards there were sluggish but steady attempts at improving navigable rivers. In practice this meant dredging out shoals, weed cutting and some bank protection with wooden poles. Such activities were usually carried out on an *ad hoc* basis by the Commissioners of Sewers (groups of local landowners appointed by the Crown) with varying degrees of success. More extensive works required either Letters Patent or an Act of Parliament. Parliamentary activity concerning navigable rivers dates back to a statute of 1424 dealing with maintenance of the River Lee.

River navigations

By the mid-sixteenth century increasing commercial pressure for the improvement of rivers was leading towards the creation of proper river navigations involving large-scale engineering, water control devices and artificial cuts bypassing the parent river. The best early example is the 'mending' of the 'Ryver of Exetor', which received its Act in 1539. This so-called canal bypassed a tricky part of the river and allowed seagoing ships to pass right up to Exeter. The work involved a 3-mile (5-km) long cut, with pound locks, and was carried out in the 1560s by John Trew of Glamorganshire, Gent. There was further work on the Lee in the 1570s and by about 1580 it was reckoned that the Thames had 23 'locks', 16 floodgates, 7 weirs and 20 watermills along its reaches between Oxford and Maidenhead. There were small-scale works taking place on other rivers in the same years. But despite these examples of Elizabethan engineering there is little evidence for a huge amount of improvement work before the seventeenth century.

By the start of the seventeenth century about 700 miles (1125km) of navigable river were available either naturally or through improvement. The demands of rising urban populations and expanding trade and industry would ensure that by 1760 a further 600 miles (965km) of waterway were added to the map of England. The first period of this development falls between 1620 and 1690; it took place in southern England and much of its impetus came from the ranks of the English gentry and merchant classes. The increased activity began with Acts of Parliament in 1605 and again in 1623 for improving the Thames. Letters Patent

15

were granted in 1619 for improving the Bristol Avon; in 1634 for the River Soar; in 1636 for the Warwickshire Avon, where William 'Waterworks' Sandys undertook the work. Sandys, like Trew, was a gentleman. So was Arnold Spencer who improved the Great Ouse. So was John Malet, improver of the Somerset Tone and Parrett. So was Andrew Yarranton, whose propagandist 'England's Improvement By Land And Sea' was published in 1677. Educated, travelled and enlightened, the ama-teur gentlemen-engineers of the seventeenth century made a significant contribution to the history of England's waterways. Several were 'undertaker-engineers': on the River Wey in the 1650s Sir Richard Weston supplied the ideas, the capital and the materials, and then directed the work himself until his death, when his son took over. With 10 locks, 4 weirs, 12 bridges and a wharf at Guildford, the Westons built the finest river navigation of the seven-teenth century (**2**).

In the second, eighteenth-century period of river navigations, the quickening pace of the economy led to the promotion of many schemes. Traders and industrialists, including maltsters,

2 *River Wey: the turf-sided lock and the low-lying, meadow-edged waterway were typical of England's early river navigations* (BW; Arthur Watts Collection).

coal owners, ironmasters and salt producers, were keen to see improvements. Between 1700 and 1760 the Stour was made navigable from Manningtree to Sudbury, the Bristol Avon from Hanham Mills to Bath, and the Kennet from Reading to Newbury. The same years saw a shift away from southern England to the Midlands and north.

The Aire & Calder was made navigable up to Leeds and Wakefield, and the Trent, the Don and the Weaver were all improved as navigations. So were the Derbyshire Derwent, the Idle, Douglas, Mersey and Irwell. But the outstanding early eighteenth-century work was still southern: the Kennet Navigation of 1718–23, engineered by John Hore, a Newbury maltster. It had 11 miles (18km) of cuts and 20 turf-sided locks.

By the middle of the eighteenth century a rising population, along with steadily expand-ing domestic markets, was demanding more food, more clothing, more raw materials and fuel. The river improvements of the seventeenth and early eighteenth centuries had contributed greatly to the growth of trade and no town or city was more than 15 miles (25km) from a navigable river or the sea. England had the best waterway system in Europe, but it was not enough. Beyond the point where navigation ended, goods had to be trans-shipped and carried by cart or on horseback. This could be difficult, expensive and inefficient. The building of a string of new turnpike roads did little to ease the problem of transporting goods, especially raw materials and coal to landlocked industries. Ironworks, potteries, brickyards and their labour forces needed coal and the coal piled up at the mines, its delivery frustrated by inadequate means of distribution. By 1760 the entrepreneurs, capital, markets, labour forces and burgeoning industry were in place and poised for a great leap forward. But the spec-tacular growth of the British economy in the second half of the eighteenth century could only take place once the coal 'famine' was lifted by the creation of a new heavy-transport

3 *Hazelhurst Locks, Caldon Canal: all the purpose-made components of canals are here fitted into a rolling landscape: stone locks with footbridges, by-weirs, and short pounds between them; a standard design accommodation bridge, with the white iron parapet of a roving bridge glimpsed beyond; a lockside hut, a lock cottage (*Derek Pratt, Waterways Photo Library*).*

4 *The Duke of Bridgewater: a mythic image of the young aristocrat pointing proudly to Barton Aqueduct. The stylised, boyish features suggest nothing of the strongly-coloured views, the risk-taking and resilient intelligence that lay behind his new commercial achievements (*BW Archives*).*

system. This was achieved by the construction of canals (**3**).

The Canal Age

Canals developed out of river navigations but they did not replace them. The two types of waterway became intertwined: linking, extending and feeding off one another. At the start of the Canal Age a fund of knowledge and experience already existed and a small number of professional or part-time navigation engineers were available to advise, make surveys or go on to canal work themselves.

The Canal Age was short — roughly from 1760 to 1840. When it began, George II was king and America was part of his empire. The population of England and Wales was about $6\frac{1}{2}$ million; Watt was developing the steam engine. When it ended, the population had risen to around 16 million, Queen Victoria ruled over vast dominions and the first steam railways were running. Transformed by unparalleled economic and industrial growth, Great Britain had become the 'workshop of the world'.

The first 'industrial' canal was the Newry Canal, built in Ireland in the 1740s to carry coal from the Tyrone mines to Dublin. It was engineered by Thomas Steers and Henry Berry who then went on to build the St Helen's Canal in England. This was really a lateral cut running parallel to and fed by the Sankey Brook. It was built in 1757 to carry coal from the St Helen's area to Liverpool. In 1759 a canal was authorized to be built from the Duke of Bridgewater's mines at Worsley to Manchester, the intention being to sell large amounts of coal cheaply but profitably. The Bridgewater Canal, built in the 1760s by John Gilbert and James Brindley, was England's first large-scale, coal-carrying canal. It was owned and paid for by the Duke of Bridgewater (**4**). In being owned by one man the Bridgewater Canal was unusual; in being financed privately, it was not.

The way in which canals were built generally followed a similar pattern: proposals would be made, support mobilised, meetings (often rowdy) would take place at an hotel or inn. An Act of Parliament would be sought, a joint-stock company formed, subscriptions invited and shares sold. Engineers and contractors would be appointed and the canal built (often in slow stages) by gangs of ungovernable labourers or 'navvies'. The opening would be celebrated with a feast of beef puddings and beer.

The short Pocklington Canal provides a vivid example of the process. Ideas for building a canal from the town of Pocklington to the river Derwent had been kicked around since the 1770s. In 1801 it was agreed at a public meeting that a canal would be of 'great Public Utility'. A brief flurry of activity was followed by a period of inaction that lasted until 1813, when Lord Fitzwilliam (who owned the Derwent) got George Leather to make a survey. Leather promptly went sick and no survey appeared until 1814, when a canal was proposed that would run from East Cottingwith to the Hull turnpike road ($^3/_4$ mile short of Pocklington) at a cost of £32,032.

A subscription was opened and 63 people (including Lord Fitzwilliam, a couple of wealthy merchants and 39 Pocklington tradesmen) raised £20,500. An Act of Parliament empowering the raising of £32,000 in £100 shares was passed in May 1815 and soon afterwards shareholders met at The Feathers in Pocklington to elect a committee. The committee confirmed Leather's appointment as engineer and agreed to 'let by ticket the cutting of the canal...in such proportions and parts as the parties choose to engage for'. The line was divided into sections and cut by different contractors between August 1816 and July 1818. It was $9^1/_2$ miles (15km) long, with nine locks and two short branches to the villages of Melbourne and Bielby. At the canal head (next to the Hull road) a basin was built with a brick 'Granary, capable of Chambering 400 quarters of Corn'. This and some adjoining wharfage were to let.

The motive behind canal building was sim-
ple: profit. The Bridgewater Canal proved dramatically profitable and the building of canals gathered momentum in the 1760s and 1770s. After a pause caused by the American War, it reached a crescendo in the Canal Mania of the 1790s. Between 1791 and 1797, 53 canals were authorized by Parliament, although not all of them were built. Canal promoters and subscribers included a real pick-and-mix of eighteenth-century society, with some investing in order to benefit as canal users, others for the financial rewards of shareholding. There were mine and quarry owners, iron-masters, pottery, glass and textile manufacturers, rich merchants, Oxford dons, solicitors, landowners, petty dukes, miscellaneous professionals and clergymen with various interests. Industrialists such as Arkwright, Boulton, Darby, Reynolds and Wedgwood threw their weight behind the promotion of canals which would benefit their businesses.

The Trent & Mersey Canal Company raised £130,000 by selling shares worth £200 each. Among the investors were the Duke of Bridgewater and some friends and relatives, some Birmingham industrialists, James Brindley and his brother, Miss Levinson-Gower, a London lady, and other locals wealthy enough to put money into the canal. Investments like this were neat and, in a business sense, incestuous. In the Mania years all kinds of people were investing in canals — small businessmen, craftsmen, tradesmen, vicars and rich widows. Most of them were locals and saw the investment as a sound one, which it often was. Some public money eventually found its way into canals: after the Napoleonic Wars government loans helped to complete the Regent's Canal and the Gloucester & Sharpness Canal. The Manchester Ship Canal was part funded with public money, and in the 1920s government finance supported the Grand Union improvements.

Companies and offices
Canals, like river navigations, were maintained and run by companies. Each company gave

5 *The seal of the Stourbridge Navigation Company: a naive drama of changeable weather, emerging industry, unloaded cargoes at a wharf and a coal boat in a lock* (BW Archives).

itself a name and a seal, which usually symbolized its commercial links and aspirations (**5**). Up to 1845, canal companies were not allowed to carry goods on their own canals and their revenue derived instead from leasing wharf, dock and warehouse space, and most importantly from the collection of tolls from goods carried. Tolls were set by a canal's Act of Parliament. The Act for the Kennet & Avon gives a typical litany of tonnages and rates: 'For all Hay, Straw, Dung, Peat, and Peatashes, and for all other Ashes intended to be used for manure, and for all Chalk, Marle, Clay, and Sand . . . the sum of One penny per ton, per mile' and so on. Tolls were collected by reliable company servants.

Canal companies tended to be small, and their employees were inevitably scattered. At the top was the shareholders' meeting which elected a management committee. The committee met regularly and decided company policy. Day-to-day running of business was left to an executive comprising, in order of seniority, a clerk (usually a solicitor), a treasurer, an accountant, an agent (or a 'general manager'), and an engineer. Below these were clerical staff, craftsmen and labourers. A cottage often went with a canal company job and companies usually owned head offices, some of which had architectural pretensions.

The Birmingham Canal office, built in 1771 in Paradise Street, was a curious, symmetrical building with an imposing octagonal centre flanked by arched gateways and end pavilions. The octagon contained the committee room: its angled windows, clocks and belfry expressed the company's vigilance over its affairs. Through the gateways lay a coal wharf, a gritty and immediate reminder of the mainstay of canal business. In Bath, in about 1810, the Kennet & Avon Canal Co. built a suave, ashlared office, which rises above the boldly rusticated portal of a short tunnel (See **1**). In the 1820s the Oxford Canal Co. moved into a Greek Revival office with a large Doric portico. The style was fashionable and appropriate to the seat of classical learning (**6**). The monumental form of the building shows how seriously this (very successful) company took itself. Most company offices were less pretentious. The Leeds & Liverpool built a modest 'canal office' (the words are carved in stone above its door) in Leeds in 1816. Inside there is a panelled meeting room. The Sleaford Navigation went for a comfortable-looking Tudor Revival house

6 *Canal House, Oxford. Designed by Richard Tawney and built in 1827–9, this serious, classical building was the head office of the Oxford Canal Co. It now forms part of St Peter's College* (RCHME Crown Copyright).

⊗ 'See' a number refer to coloured plates between pp 64 & 65.

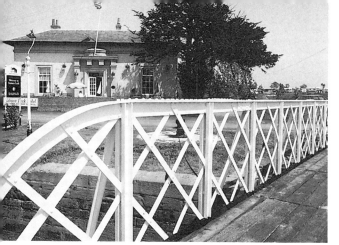

7 Banqueting house and big river equipment at Naburn Locks, River Ouse. Regency architecture of the 1820s. Authority with a light touch; this is where the bosses dined.

in stone, the Stourbridge Canal Co. for an 1849 brick and terracotta block, unassumingly attached to some cottages. The Bridgewater, Bradford, Chester, and Gloucester & Berkeley companies all chose rather bland, 'off-the-peg' buildings. Beech House on the Llangollen, built in 1806, is a domestic-looking company office on a rural canal.

8 Clock tower, Northwich: a useful ornament at the former head office of the worthy Weaver Navigation Trust. Built in 1830, rebuilt by British Waterways in the 1990s (D. Pratt, Waterways Photo Library).

River navigation offices tended to be more exuberant than those on canals. The Ouse Navigation built itself a stylish banqueting house in 1823 at Naburn, next to the big locks (7). The Conservators of the Cam followed suit with a jaunty, Dutch-gabled house of 1842, furnished with a committee room and extensive cellars. At Northwich a free-standing clock-tower with a cupola was placed alongside the solid-looking head office of the Weaver Navigation Trust (8). The smallest canal and navigation companies who could not afford, and did not require, purpose-built headquarters made do with a room at an inn or rented premises. The Warwick & Birmingham Canal Co. took on a house in Birmingham in 1793 and instructed their clerk to fit out a committee room with 'a skirting Board . . . a Hearth Stone, and Chimney piece to the same. To build a Brewhouse, Privy and Wall, to make the yard and Garden private and entire'. A well was to be sunk and a water pump provided; 'the room to be occupied as an Office' was to be properly glazed and 'twelve Chairs, a Table, Window Blinds and Curtains' were to be bought to furnish the place.

England's canals can be separated into different types. Some linked major river navigations and were wide enough to take barges. Others, particularly in the Midlands, were narrow and took specially designed narrow boats. At one end of the scale there were broad ship canals for coasting and deep-water craft; at the other there were all-terrain tub boat canals. Within these main types there was much local and regional variety. In architectural and engineering terms three overlapping phases, or 'ways of doing things', can be identified: Pioneering from c. 1760 to 1780; Heroic from c. 1780 to 1835; and Late from 1835 onwards.

Pioneering canals

With the exception of the Bridgewater Canal, Pioneering canals were cheap, usually narrow, and compared with later canals, easy to build. They were earth-hugging, contour-trailing canals whose engineering had a going-along-with-nature look. Those winding canals like the old Birmingham Canal, the Oxford, the Wyrley & Essington (known as the 'Curly Wyrley') had a Georgian craftsman's feel to them. In their sinuous routes and the curving shapes of their lock beams, bridge-holes and parapets there were rustic echoes of landscape gardening, Chippendale chairs and Wedgwood pots. Unselfconsciously they partook of a tradition that was eighteenth-century, English and beautiful.

The engineers of the early canals were led by Brindley, 'as plain a looking man as one of the boors of the Peak', who 'handles rocks as easily as you would plum-pies'. There is a myth that Brindley could hardly read or write and stayed in bed to solve problems. In reality he was an ambitious businessman and an inventive engineer, modelling aqueducts in cheese and reputedly digging a trial lock in his back garden. Brindley made a name for himself thanks to the Duke of Bridgewater and the 'team' (the term is used loosely) of assistant engineers he gathered around him: his brother-in-law Hugh Henshall, his apprentice Robert Whitworth, Thomas Dadford the elder and Samuel Simcock. Brindley acted as a consultant on most of the early canals, but he only actually saw through, entirely on his own, parts of the Bridgewater and the Trent & Mersey.

Brindley, and others in his team, pioneered engineering which played safe and took few risks. Large numbers of locks strung out along a canal were a typical feature and were part of the refusal to find more daring and more expensive solutions. River valley routes were favoured, embankments and cuttings avoided if at all possible. Aqueducts were low, squat and oversized, tunnels were narrow, wonky and only built if there was no alternative. Building narrow canals kept costs down and saved water. Canals of the 1760s and 1770s, like the Birmingham, Chesterfield, Coventry, Droitwich, Oxford, Trent & Mersey and Staffordshire & Worcestershire, exhibit many Pioneer

ing features. They were experimental, but successful. They helped establish the conditions under which new engineering methods, structures and building types could be developed.

Heroic canals

Heroic antecedents are seen in Pioneering works dating from the 1770s and 1780s, such as John Longbotham's great Leeds & Liverpool locks, the straight lines of John Smeaton's Birmingham & Fazeley Canal, the coast-to-coast Forth & Clyde and the weird stone architecture of the Thames & Severn. But a Heroic 'style' only emerged strongly between *c*. 1790 and 1820: the dangerous, atmospheric years of Napoleonic War and Canal Mania. It is stamped with the imaginative, large-scale planning and inspired leadership of engineers like William Jessop, George Leather, John Rennie and Thomas Telford. Its characteristics include direct routes, deep cuttings, huge embankments, wide channels, long summits, locks in groups or flights and the use of prefabricated components and new technology.

Where Pioneering canals went along with nature, Heroic began to go against it: up and down and straight through, instead of round and round. It was fine, dramatic stuff. Canals climbed through the landscape, cut through rock, tunnelled beneath hills and spanned river valleys. They linked great towns and cities, sending water where it had no natural right to be. The very idea of building a canal across the Pennines was heroic, yet by 1816 there were three; the Rochdale, Huddersfield Narrow and Leeds & Liverpool. In the Midlands, Jessop's Grand Junction ploughed its way towards London. In the south, Rennie joined the Kennet and Avon Navigations by means of a broad, barge-carrying canal, distinguished by massive, classically-detailed aqueducts. England's first ship canal, the Gloucester & Sharpness, revived the port of Gloucester. The Lancaster Canal opened up north-west Lancashire. The Worcester & Birmingham, Grand Western, Cromford, Peak Forest, Llangollen, Macclesfield and

9 *Thomas Telford: engineer, architect, poet and Scotsman of winning ways. The print suggests something of the relentless energy, the ideas, imagination, and ambition of this great form-giver (*BW Archives*).*

Shropshire Union can all be considered Heroic canals. In Scotland the majestic Caledonian Canal linked the North Sea with the Atlantic Ocean.

The best engineers of 1790 to 1835 had the simple ability to design one thing after another. Rennie and Telford (**9**) attended to everything from aqueducts to gudgeon pins, and there were essential components — bridges, lock gates, mile-posts — that could be 'mass produced' in easily-repeated forms. There was a desire to get things right and make them look right too. There is the same delight in clarity and order on the pages of Telford's *Atlas* as in a Wedgwood pot catalogue. There is the same tendency, too, to standardization linked with an unerring instinct for quality. Quality is a hallmark of this period. Nowhere is it more in evidence than on the Shropshire Union of 1826–35, where the Canal Age reached its

zenith. This was the last full-scale canal built in England by traditional methods. Its clean, sweeping lines, long straight lengths and huge embankments and cuttings are splendid. Its planning and engineering are superb, but it came too late to be a model for anything except railway building.

Late canals

Late canals were usually attempts at reshaping earlier waterways or were built to avoid old congested lines. Telford's Birmingham New Main Line completed in 1838 led the way: crisp and straight, with twin-arched bridges, double towpaths and a wide channel with walled sides. Its proprietors boasted that it was 'second to no other Canal Works whatever in the Kingdom'. Many of the last canals were built as branches and extensions to the BCN (Birmingham Canal Navigations), which remained busy despite the newly-arrived railways. BCN canals of the 1840s include the Stourbridge Extension, Bentley, Rushall, Walsall Junction, and the Hatherton and Titford branches. The Tame Valley Canal, built as an avoiding line, was kept straight and level by means of deep cutting and colossal embankments, one of which took it across the seven-year-old London and Birmingham Railway (**10**). In the 1850s the Droitwich Junction Canal, the Cannock Extension Canal, the Anglesey Branch and the Netherton Tunnel Line were cut. Away in the West Country the heavily-engineered Chard Canal opened in 1842, only to be abandoned in 1867. The Don was greatly improved and a painful stretch of the river Calder was bypassed by George Leather. The Aire & Calder's locks were enlarged from the 1850s to the 1880s. Between 1871 and 1897 the Weaver Navigation was magnificently rebuilt by E. Leader Williams. The New Junction Canal, austere and straight as an arrow, was opened as late as 1905.

This summary sounds impressive; but though the Late phase produced some excellent engineering it did not amount to many miles of new

10 *Tame Valley Canal cutting: wholly man-made, dead straight and crossed by high-level bridges. One of England's lean, Late phase canals of the 1840s (*BW; Arthur Watts Collection*).*

waterway. There was one grand exception: the Manchester Ship Canal, a one-off, whose sheer size and methods of construction make it quite different from any other waterway. It turned Manchester into a major port, but by the time it opened in 1894 England was already crisscrossed by 20,000 miles (32,000km) of railway line.

Decline and revival

Railways were a Georgian invention: the first steam locomotive was built in 1801; the Stockton and Darlington Railway opened in 1825;

23

the Liverpool and Manchester in 1830; the London and Birmingham in 1837. In the 1830s there were still more miles of canal built than railways; in 1845, England went railway mad. The realization that goods and passengers could now be carried at speed over great distances fired the imagination. The commercial and industrial potential seemed limitless. Railway engineers threw themselves into a fury, designing and building a brave new world. The impact on canals was dramatic. After 1845, their importance declined. A few crumpled before the onslaught, others were sold out or were taken over by railway companies. Several small canals simply closed down and vanished. The Andover, Carlisle, Croydon and Glastonbury canals were converted into railway lines. Long-distance, agriculture-related canals suffered most; short-haul canals which delivered coal to the factory or mill door in industrial areas suffered least. But once railways had got a grip on the country there was little incentive to invest in canals, and those which remained in business usually saw dwindling receipts and at best a long-drawn out decline. Attempts to reorganize and fight back were bedevilled by a history of localism, non-cooperation and a lack of uniformity in gauges and equipment.

The Great War of 1914–18 saw a further decline in commercial carrying. In 1898 canals had carried 39 million tons of goods per year (while railways carried 378 million tons). In 1919 they carried 22 million, in 1938 only 13 million. There were more closures during the period between the two World Wars. During the Second World War, despite some much-publicized remodelling of the Grand Union Canal, another 200 miles (320km) of waterway were abandoned by Act of Parliament.

The founding of a pressure group, the Inland Waterways Association, in 1946, and nationalization in 1947 were two different reactions to the problem of run-down or derelict waterways. Later came the recognition of their amenity and redevelopment value. England's canals have been largely rescued by the growth of one industry which their builders never foresaw — the leisure industry. Today it is possible to travel by boat from London to the Midlands, or to Bath, or Chester, or Manchester, or even by devious courses to York, Gloucester and Lincoln. From a slowly moving boat England's landscapes take on a different meaning. Simple words like 'tree', 'water' and 'hedge' begin to stir the imagination. Different waterways take in the scenic excitement of Wales and the Pennines or the flat, extended agriculture of the Fens, or the jigsaw of towns, villages and fields in between: those Midlands' landscapes which were shaped by the canals and by the wharfs and factories which spread along their banks — potteries, iron, glass, brick, lime and gas works, coal mines and foundries, and batteries of cotton mills, maltings, breweries and warehouses. There are hundreds of early nineteenth-century prints displaying a proud factory with smoking chimneys and a boat on a canal in the foreground. Most of those factories have gone. Many canal buildings have been lost. But those that remain, or can be rediscovered through archives, maps and photographs, represent a unique record, an architectural history of a people transforming themselves from an agricultural to an industrial nation — the first nation ever to do so.

2

Infrastructure

Canal architecture is the architecture of work, experiment and revolution. What is now precious and idyllic was once hewn out in the service of industry: brick, stone, wood, iron and

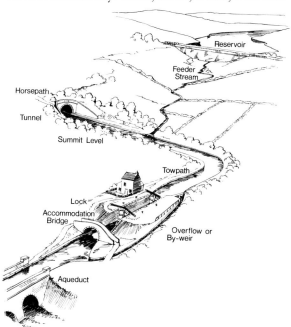

11 *How a canal works* (P. Dunn).

water urgently fitted together to form still-water routes where horses could pull loaded boats. It is important to remember how artificial canals are: they literally had to be cut through the landscape. The infrastructure of canals — how they were built, equipped, supplied with water and maintained is the subject of this chapter (**11**, **12**).

Canal construction

Simple, straightforward sweat built England's canals. There were no mechanical aids, the work was hard, often dangerous, and usually took years to complete. Ideally the best possible line for a canal would be topographically sound and would link towns, coalfields, ironworks and other industries *en route*. Special attention would be paid to natural obstacles and changes of level, as well as to gentlemen's parks, houses, gardens, orchards, mills, roads and so on (**13**). Before any work began a principal engineer was appointed and surveys were made. Surveying was carried out by triangulation using a theodolite, a long chain, a spirit level with telescopic sights and wooden poles with sliding

12 *Constructing a canal* (P. Dunn).

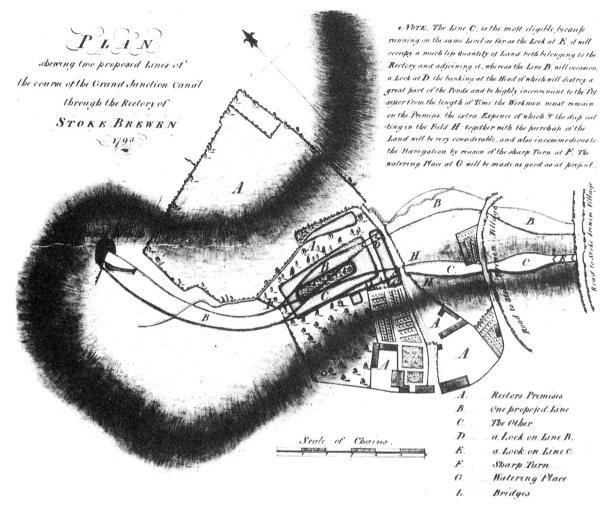

NOTE. The Line C. is the most eligible, because running on the same Level as far as the Lock at E. it will occupy a much less Quantity of Land both belonging to the Rectory and adjoining it, whereas the Line B. will occasion a Lock at D. the banking at the Head of which will destroy a great part of the Ponds, and be highly inconvenient to the Possessor from the length of Time the Workmen must remain on the Premises, the extra Expence of which & the deep cutting in the Field H. together with the purchase of the Land will be very considerable, and also incommodious to the Navigation by reason of the sharp Turn at F. The watering Place at G. will be made as good as at present.

Scale of Chains.

A.	Rectors Premises
B.	One proposed Line
C.	The Other
D.	a Lock on Line B.
E.	a Lock on Line C.
F.	Sharp Turn
G.	Watering Place
h.	Bridges

13 *Canal construction meant disruption: a 1793 plan of two proposed lines for cutting the Grand Junction (now Grand Union) Canal through Stoke Bruerne rectory. Parkland, hedges, gardens and ponds typify the enclosed fabric of the Georgian countryside. Many landowners were hostile to the invasion of their well-ordered estates by canals (BW Archives).*

marks. Without contour maps and with only a rudimentary knowledge of geology, it was complicated work. Surveys were often accompanied by drawings showing different routes and details. After 1793, Parliament required a complete plan for any canal seeking an Act. Engineers would often prepare books of drawings for standardized or important structures, such as bridges, locks (**14**), tunnels and aque-

ducts. These drawings, colourwashed in pale peach, buff or pink can be very beautiful and clear. Jessop, Rennie and Telford all produced exquisite signed drawings.

The principal engineer usually left a resident engineer and his assistants in charge of the cutting and digging. Following a survey, the line of a canal would be pegged out, topsoil removed and sections let to contractors or 'hagmasters' who employed local labourers, often farmworkers who downed tools at harvesttime and went back to the land. Some canal companies employed direct labour, and by the 1790s there is evidence for migratory gangs of navigators, or so-called navvies, who worked only on canals. They brought their labour; the canal companies supplied tools, barrows,

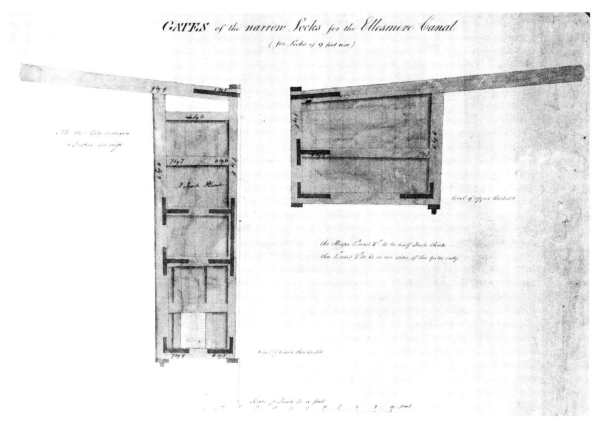

GATES of the narrow Locks for the Ellesmere Canal

(for Locks of 9 feet rise)

14 *Lock gates for the Ellesmere (now Llangollen) Canal: the careful, clear-cut drawings made by canal engineers* (BW Archives).

wheeling planks and horsing blocks. In the Heroic phase big contractors specializing in canal work and in aqueduct and tunnel construction appeared. These firms were not always reliable — the Lancaster Canal company's employment of Pinkerton and Murray led to complaints, bitterness and halted work. In the end the company reverted to a number of more easily managed small contractors. Building canals was a risky business.

Spades, shovels and pickaxes were used to dig out the shapes of reservoirs, locks, bridge and aqueduct foundations, drains, culverts, safety-gates, weirs, winding-holes and basins. Digging out a lock chamber required skill and supervision. The canal bed and sides were made watertight by lining or 'puddling' with a thick, clayey mixture of loam and coarse sand. This was beaten, chopped and watered into a semi-fluid state, then trodden down by heavy horses or workmen wearing puddling-boots. Wherever possible, suitable puddling material, gravel for surfacing locksides, towpaths and wharfs, and brick earth for on-site brickmaking were dug out of the canal bed itself.

Towpaths were banked up using spoil from the same excavations. A model towpath was 2ft 6in (0.75m) above water level and slightly cambered away from the water's edge. It had foundations of stone and rubble and was tamped down and covered with gravel, a stone shingle called raffle or a mix of ashes and crushed cinders. On the immediate approaches to a lock or a bridge the towpath was stone or brick-paved and where a brickway dived beneath a bridge it was formed with ribs of raised scorchers to help horses keep their footing. Lock flights on busy urban stretches of canal were paved for some distance. There was much experiment with thick and quickset hedges in Pioneering years, and the ideal cattle-proof hedge was judged to be whitethorn raised on a low embankment, with a ditch on either side. In towns, hedges gave way to factory or purpose-built towpath walls. Some stripey lengths of the latter survive on urban stretches of the Worcester & Birmingham. For the most part, banks were left natural or faced up with brushwood, as horse-boats created little wash. Later, dry stone pitching and brick appeared for improved urban canals like the BCN. Concrete and steel piling are modern methods of bank protection, dating back to the 1930s.

15 *A deep and silent cutting driven like a wedge through the countryside: 'the Rockin' (or Woodseaves Cutting) Shropshire Union Canal (*BW; Arthur Watts Collection*).*

Cuttings and embankments

The biggest site works on a canal were earth-moving jobs: digging the channel itself, and forming cuttings and embankments to keep it level through uneven terrain. A cutting is a way of lowering a canal summit (which improves water supply) and of gaining a shorter route between places. Pioneering canals avoided deep cuttings; Heroic canals went for them, despite the trouble and expense involved in their construction. The slopes had to be of the right gradient to avoid slips and this was difficult to achieve. Excavation meant the erection of scaffolds, horse gins and runs of swaying wheeling planks, by which means loaded barrows were either hoisted or pushed and pulled out of the cutting. According to Jessop it was best to begin at both ends of a cutting, as he

did at Tring on the Grand Union. Tring is a fine example; as are Burbage Cutting on the Kennet & Avon, and Galton Cutting on the BCN. The Bridgwater & Taunton Canal has a small but unusual cutting, given architectural treatment by having high-walled sides (See **2**). On the Tame Valley Canal there are grim cuttings shadowed by massive embankments — examples of cut-and-fill technique, where spoil excavated from a cutting is used to build an embankment. This was an Heroic development and was brought to perfection by Telford on the Shropshire Union (**15**).

Embankments were eschewed by most early canal builders. The Bridgewater Canal, though, is a notable exception in this. Contour canals, like the Staffs & Worcester and the Oxford, have low embankments raised by stubbornly digging earth out of the neighbouring fields — leaving ditches cut along either side of the canal. A less wasteful method was the formation of half-embanked terraces where the canal line clawed its way along the side of a valley. The Cromford, Lancaster and Leicester Line illustrate this most effectively in places. In Cheshire, the Trent & Mersey has terraced stretches high above the River Weaver.

Big free-standing embankments, like deep cuttings, are Heroic features. Jessop noted that they should be built early in a canal's construction so as to allow time to consolidate. His own embankments at Weedon and Wolverton on the Grand Union will stand comparison with most. Their great sloping sides are penetrated by underbridges: short tunnels which take minor roads, streams and cattle creeps beneath the canal. Such features occur on the Llangollen, the Leeds & Liverpool and the Tame Valley Canal and variously on the northern Oxford, the western Kennet & Avon, the Macclesfield and the Birmingham New Main Line. The Shropshire Union has spectacular embankments at Nantwich, Shebdon and Shelmore (**16**), interrupted by cast-iron aqueducts and punched through with stone-arched road tunnels, finished with sloping wing walls

16 *Shelmore 'Great Bank' reveals the grandeur of the Shropshire Union Canal. Trees stabilise the steep banks. Down below lie fields and a lane (*BW; Arthur Watts Collection*).*

to prevent slips. Slippage was the greatest problem encountered by embankment builders. Shelmore 'Great Bank', rising above quiet fields with the blue hills of Wales in the distance, was built to avoid disturbing the pheasants of Norbury Park. Its construction was a nightmare: time and again the sides slipped and had to be re-stabilized. It took six years to finish and delayed the opening of the canal; it stands as a poignant earthen monument on the last of the navvy-built canals.

Flash locks and staunches

Cuttings and embankments kept a canal summit flat. But away from the summit a canal steps downwards and the most common method of overcoming the changes in level was to build locks. Historically there were two main types of locks: flash locks, of which surviving remains are scanty (and which were not built on canals), and pound locks, which survive in large numbers and exhibit many regional and local variations of shape, size and equipment.

The first locks, which were built on river navigation systems like those of the Thames,

17 *A Thames flash-lock; ragged, flimsy-looking and wooden. The man is raising the paddles; after that he will pull aside the beam he is standing on to let a boat through. Drawn by H.R. Robertson, an early waterways tourist* (BW Archives).

Severn and Fens, were flash locks. They date back to the Middle Ages and despite being inefficient and troublesome were still in use in the early twentieth century. They allowed boats to negotiate shallows, or to pass through weirs built for other purposes, and came in two types: a beam and paddle lock which was usually kept closed, and a staunch which was usually kept open. Beam and paddle locks were usually built into part of a milling weir across a river. Early examples were picturesque, complicated affairs whose wooden parts needed constant maintenance (**17**). Later they were tidied up and given permanent-looking stone abutments and iron components. They consisted of a framework of two beams, one lying across the river bed, the other at water level, with vertical planks called paddles and rimers slotted through them, effectively providing a gate which held back the water. To let a boat through, the paddles were pulled up and the water-level beam pulled aside. A flash of water was released and the boat rode downstream upon it. The passage upstream was less exhilarating: winches, sweating horses and men had to haul a boat against the current. Once a boat had passed, the lock had to be reassembled.

Staunches were more reliable and came in the form of a gate staunch, which acted like a single pair of lock gates; a guillotine staunch, which was common in East Anglia and is found in modern form on the Nene and Great Ouse; and a plank staunch, basically planks of wood dropped into masonry slots to form a dam.

Flash locks were not economical. They wasted water, eroded banks and delayed upstream traffic. Although not found on canals, because water wastage would have been catastrophic, they played a vital part in the evolution of the pound lock, which was suitable for both river navigations and canals. Two staunches set close together created an embryonic pound lock; early examples where the pound is merely a turf-sided continuation of the river are clearly descended from flash locks.

Pound locks
Primitive pound locks appeared on the Exeter Canal in the 1560s. These had lengthy earth banks between vertically rising gates. There were shorter pound locks with mitred gates on the Lee in the 1570s, their design probably influenced by technology developed in Italy and the Low Countries. Pound locks began to replace flash locks on other river navigations in the seventeenth century. They were introduced on the Thames in the 1630s, although curiously they never superseded flash locks altogether. Turf-sided locks were built on the Wey in the mid-seventeenth century and on the Kennet in the early eighteenth century. In their final form they consisted of masonry head and tail walls, wooden gates and sloping earth sides with wooden or iron guard rails. Locks on river navigations were rarely of uniform dimensions. Most were rectangular but there were diamond, circular and half-moon pounds shaped to suit uneven banks. Turf-sided locks waste water and even on well-supplied rivers tended to be rebuilt with walls of dry or roughly-squared stone, and later ashlared stone or brick. On canals, where water supply is crucial, locks were constructed with stone or brick chambers from the beginning.

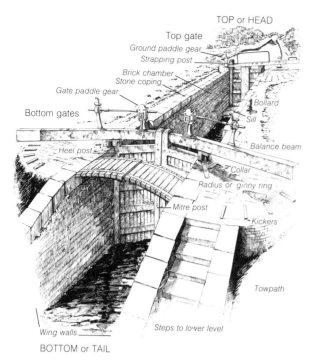

TOP or HEAD
Top gate
Ground paddle gear
Strapping post
Brick chamber
Stone coping
Gate paddle gear
Bottom gates
Bollard
Sill
Heel post
Balance beam
Collar
Radius or ginny ring
Mitre post
Kickers
Towpath
Wing walls
Steps to lower level
BOTTOM or TAIL

18 *The parts of a typical canal lock (*P. Dunn*).*

A typical canal lock consists of the following: a rectangular chamber of brick or stone, finished with flat stone copings; heavy wooden gates balanced by wooden beams (which also act as levers), each gate anchored by a collar and turning on a cast-iron pin in a pot, the whole thing held in place by water pressure; and hand-worked paddle gear mounted on a gate or on a stand set in the ground nearby (**18**).

Broad locks have two pairs of mitred gates with the mitre pointing against the water pressure; a narrow lock has one pair at its tail and a single gate at its head, or else a single gate at each end. Some locks were built with guillotine gates, such as those on the Shrewsbury Canal (**22**). Gates and beams (which are of wood or steel or occasionally cast iron) are usually black, with beam ends picked out in white. The use of paint, tar and whitewash to preserve gates and make them visible in grey weather or the dark is derived from nautical traditions.

Most locks have been rebuilt and had their demountable equipment (gates, gate fittings, paddle gear) renewed many times over and there is now almost no such thing as an 'original' lock. But old prints, photographs and the retention of local styles provide examples of the rich variety which existed when each company had its own distinctive accessories.

Paddle gear

Paddle gear consists of the hand-worked mechanisms that allow water into and out of a lock

19 *An early way of opening and closing gate paddles: former peg-and-pull gear on the River Wey* (BW Archives).

by means of hatches cut in gates or by sluices — brick, or stone-lined drains — cut into the chamber walls. Typically, a lock has ground paddles at its head gates and gate paddles on its tail gates. The gearing is mounted on stands or jacks of iron, stone or wood.

Early paddle gear, especially on river navigations, was often of the peg-and-pull or handspike type, usually moved up and down by brute force (**19**). Rack and pinion gear, a more common eighteenth-century innovation, has

20a *Oxford Canal gate gear: a rack and pinion mounted on a cast iron jack and operated via a 'banjo' reduction box* (BW; Arthur Watts Collection).

20b *Pivoting paddle boards worked by long winding racks: Leeds and Liverpool Canal* (BW; Arthur Watts Collection).

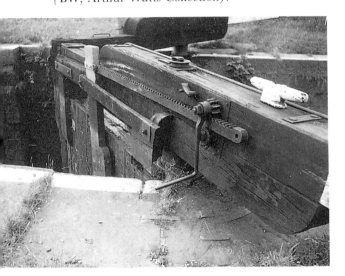

counterweights on the Bridgwater & Taunton (**21**). Further variety is found in the equipment used to work locks on river navigations: manual capstans and bulky, boxed-in winches to open big gates; Pelton gears (like those on the Weaver) with their wheel-work placed in a covered well; gate gear operated by turning a hand-wheel. Paddle gear ironmongery, including cogs, racks, catch-wheels and jacks, was usually cast at local foundries or at large company maintenance yards. Sometimes the date or the company initials were stamped into the castings. Many of the late nineteenth-century refurbishments carried out under Thomas Millner on the Grand Union were marked in this way.

Lock technology developed quickly as engineers became used to handling large volumes of water in cramped spaces. Yet in the Pioneering years the important principles of uniformity in size and spacing were not at first recognized. The Louth Canal was built with locks of different sizes (with chambers of scalloped brick bays, creating a very strong wall). Other canals were cut in a way that necessitated a lock here, another there, and so on. Heroic locks were grouped, where possible, at either end of a long level or summit: the Leicester

21 *Ball and chain counterweighted paddle gear: local style on the Bridgwater & Taunton Canal* (R. Butler).

remained in use up to the present. Worm and nut devices or side paddles are rarer, although examples survive on the Leeds & Liverpool. Twentieth-century rationalization, including the introduction of hydraulic gear, has eroded local flavour and idiosyncracy and a connoisseur's eye is needed to spot old company replicas and survivals (**20**a and b): crown wheel and pinion sets on the Oxford; double-toothed racks on the Grand Union; handspike sets on the Calder & Hebble; shrouded reduction boxes on the Shropshire Union; and ball-and-chain

Line is a good example. On the Rochdale and Shropshire Union, locks were built with a uniform rise and standardized parts for easy replacement and maintenance. On trans-Pennine canals, lockage was very heavy: 91 in 127 miles (205km) on the Leeds & Liverpool; 92 in 33 miles (53km) on the Rochdale; 74 in 20 miles (32km) on the Huddersfield Narrow.

22 Eyton on Weald Lock, Shrewsbury Canal: guillotine bottom gate on a 1790s tub-boat canal, now derelict. One of 11 narrow locks, each taking 4 five-ton boats (BW; Arthur Watts Collection).

The main function of a lock is to overcome changing levels, but at the same time some locks fulfilled other purposes. A stop lock links one canal to another and usually has a rise of no more than a few inches and gates which open in either direction. There are good examples at Hawkesbury Junction, at Lapworth, and at King's Norton, which has rare guillotine gates. There are locks which let boats into basins and docks. River locks like those at Newbury, Selby,

Stourport and Gloucester link canals with river navigations. A sea lock, which is rarer, links a canal with a harbour, as can be seen at Bude.

Risers and flights

Architectural quality and hydrological excitement are found where locks are grouped tightly together forming a flight, or else were built one immediately above another forming a riser or staircase. Risers were a Pioneering invention. The finest examples are Bingley Three Rise, Bingley Five Rise (John Longbotham's 'Great Lock') on the Leeds & Liverpool (**23**). Built by local masons, the scale of these stone locks is breathtaking. Water cascades over gates (and through sluices) from one chamber to the next and boats can be quickly let up or down. Other examples include Grindley Brook on the Llangollen, with its long horse ramps, and the chunky-looking Bunbury Locks and the steeply-descending Chester Locks, both on the Shropshire Union, the latter partly hacked through

23 Bingley Five Rise, Leeds and Liverpool Canal: a great staircase charging up a hill. Big stones, big gates; tough details on a scale rarely seen on canals. Completed as early as 1774 by local Yorkshiremen. (R. Butler)

24 *Changing levels and textures: Bratch Locks, Staffs & Worcester Canal; an early Brindley staircase later altered to its present cluttered appearance.*

solid rock. England's greatest staircase stands at one end of the Grand Union's Leicester Line, where in 1810 Benjamin Bevan began Foxton Locks: two five-rises which charge up a hillside, the ground humped and ramped around the strong vertical and horizontal lines of their equipment (see **3**). At the other end Bevan built Watford Locks (rebuilt in 1905), a flight and staircase combination set on a bend, which takes the canal down to the Grand Union main line level. Risers waste water; this explains the terraced side-ponds at Foxton. It probably also explains Bratch Locks on the Staffs & Worcester (**24**), where a very early two-lock riser of *c.* 1770 was later turned into a strange, squashed flight of three locks with large curling side ponds.

A flight is a series of ordinary locks, each separated from the next by a short pound. Flights enable canals to make lengthy climbs out of valleys and are characteristic of watershed-crossing Heroic canals. There are examples hidden in the maze of the BCN

plateau, like Stourbridge Locks, which date from 1779, and Perry Barr Locks, which date from the 1840s. Walsall Locks are a flight of eight, as are Delph Locks, which James Walker built in 1858 to replace a less efficient flight of nine built by Thomas Dadford the elder in the 1770s. Walker used Dadford's old top and bottom locks but slotted six new ones in between. Dadford's locks meandered and had side ponds; Walker's go up in a straight line — these are Late locks, whose engineering bricks, sharp stonework and hard lines carry real conviction. In Bath, the Kennet & Avon Canal leaves the river by wide locks which clamber past genteel backyards and gardens. Further east on the same canal, the Caen Hill Flight — a solemn regiment of 29 locks with side-ponds — carries boats up the long hill to Devizes and the summit. Caen Hill is a remarkable achievement. In 1811 one of the Kennet & Avon's first enthusiasts described the flight as 'a most curious and striking instance of the wonderful perfection to which the art of Engineering has been carried in this country'.

The Leeds & Liverpool has a wandering flight of 23 broad locks at Wigan, the Worcester & Birmingham has a flight of 30 locks at Tardebigge. Most of the above mentioned lock flights are built of brick. But on the Peak Forest Canal between 1801 and 1804, Benjamin Outram built Marple Locks of millstone grit. The visual appeal of these locks lies in the sheer vigour of their engineering: the clarity with which lock walls run slap into tail bridges; the lively effect of one lock effortlessly taking over from another; the way in which silent tons of water are held in check by stone and timber. In terms of original fabric and accessories, the most complete flight is 'The Golden Steps to Heaven' at Hatton on the Grand Union. This was built in the 1930s with precast concrete and tough-looking blue bricks. The locks have crisp, shipshape details and the shrouded paddle gear (called 'candlesticks' by boatmen) has the pleasing look and feel of marine equipment.

Locking up or down a canal constantly takes water away from the summit. One way to save water was to cut a small reservoir or side pond alongside a lock. Typically this consisted of a sunken brick or stone tank, usually square in shape and connected to the lock chamber by a culvert which was opened and closed by a paddle. Descending boats divert water from the lock into the side pond until both are equal and then close the paddle. Ascending boats use the same water to help refill the lock. This saves half a lockful of water each time. Side ponds are often found in conjunction with flights (like Caen Hill) and staircases, although earlier examples (like Bingley Five Rise) do not have them. There are numerous single examples along the Grand Union, where they were first experimented with in 1803 by the great lock-maker Bevan. Paired or double locks (two ordinary locks placed side by side) fulfil a similar function and also speed up traffic. The busy Regent's Canal was built with double locks in the 1820s and a group were built at Hillmorton on the Oxford Canal during the 1830s' improvements.

A lock is an assemblage, a 'kit of parts'. Many of the strongest images of locks are associated with their details: the pattern made by slatted planks on a gate; the half-violin-shaped step on a balance beam or the 'sailor's hat' on a strapping post; plank-ways and narrow footbridges across tails; the bony, clearly expressed shapes of paddle gear; the scuffed bricks of heel grips or 'ginny rings'.

Until recently it was still possible to find, in canal yards around England, well-thumbed exercise books with the workmanlike words 'Carpenter's Lock Gate Book' written on the front cover. In these books page after dog-eared page have large drawings of the gates which belong to each lock on the canal, with dimensions, measurements and other notes carefully marked. No two locks are ever exactly alike and these dusty scrapbooks of drawings were an essential and simple way of getting things right. Everything at a lockside is there for a purpose. There is no unnecessary clutter in the neat angles, slopes, corners, robust balance beams (originally rough-hewn) and well-worn brickways. These things, along with the subdued colours and textures and changing views — from a boat, from the lockside, from the foot-bridge — combine to make a lock the most emblematic of canal structures.

25 *An inclined plane engine house from R. Fulton's 1796* Treatise on the Improvement of Canal Navigation. *The severe, temple-like shed (a form which haunted much eighteenth-century architectural theory) here provides shelter and a framework for the 'engine'; bucket-in-a-well machinery which counterbalances a tub-boat (*BW Archives*).*

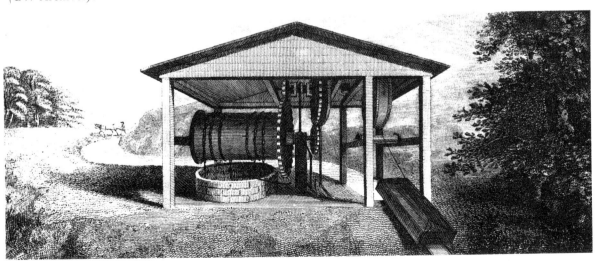

26 *Foxton inclined plane; an effective but ultimately abortive attempt to get big barges moving between the Thames and the Trent. Its site is now derelict* (BW Archives).

Inclined planes and lifts

Locks were not the only way of changing levels on a canal: from the 1780s onwards mechanical alternatives to long flights of locks and heavy wastage of water were sought. The essential idea was to move boats up and down by means of a lift or an inclined plane. Of the two, inclined planes proved more workable. Robert Fulton published some examples (**25**) in his enthusiastic *Treatise on the Improvement of Canal Navigation* (1796) and as early as 1788 William Reynolds had built a simple inclined plane on the short Ketley Canal. He repeated the success by building three others on the Shropshire Canal in the 1790s. Telford wrote: 'The inclined planes, the small boats, the ascending and descending . . . with the various machinery connected therewith upon the Ketley and Shropshire Canals . . . were each of them new with regard to British canal-making . . . .' The Hay inclined plane, which carried tub boats between the Shropshire Canal and wharfs on the Severn, is now part of the Ironbridge Gorge Museum. It worked by raising boats onto wooden trolleys running on two iron railway tracks. Loaded boats were winched into position at the top by means of a rope drum powered by a small steam engine. They then descended by gravity and acted as counterweights to draw unladen boats upwards on the other track. A boat could

be raised 207ft (63m) in $3\frac{1}{2}$ minutes.

In the south-west peninsula, where water supply was a great problem, there were inclined planes on the Rolle, the Chard and on the Bude Canal, which had six, using tub-boats with wheels fitted to their hulls. These were built by James Green. Five of them were waterwheel-powered; the sixth at Hobbacott Down worked on a bucket-in-a-well system. Last and greatest of the inclines was Foxton, on the Leicester Line of the Grand Union (**26**). Built in 1900 on a steep site, it consisted of two large counterbalancing tanks, which ran on rails and were powered by a steam engine. The incline was a success. It worked well, saved water, and took 12 minutes to transfer a boat from one level to another. Foxton was part of a scheme to use the Leicester Line as a through-route for barges travelling between the Thames and the Trent. But without a similar incline at the Watford end of the line the scheme was useless. By 1910 the incline was disused; by 1928 it had been scrapped and boats reverted to the 80-minute scramble through Foxton Locks.

Vertical lifts were experimented with at various times from the late eighteenth century. Some of the designs were daft and dangerous. Others were let down by defective materials and machinery as wheels and pulleys buckled under loads, chains strained and snapped, and huge iron buckets hurtled down well-shafts. Despite the air of unreality which haunted the subject, James Green designed and built seven vertical lifts on the Grand Western Canal before his sudden dismissal in 1836. His lifts worked for 30 problematic years before the canal closed. Green's lifts each consisted of two counterbalancing caissons. The biggest of them rose 42ft 6in (13m), but this was small by comparison with the terrifying 'hydrostatick' lift which Robert Weldon had built at Combe Hay on the Somerset Coal Canal in 1796. This required a boat and its crew to enter a watertight iron coffin which rode inside a tremendous 88ft (27m) deep pit. The lift worked until its walls began to collapse inwards and it had to be

27 *Anderton boat lift: massively confident High Victorian engineering, dreamt up and designed by E. Leader Williams (BW Archives).*

abandoned.

Remains of inclined planes typically include tumbled, overgrown masonry and odd holes in the ground. Lift remains, with one great exception, are almost non-existent. The exception is Anderton boat lift (**27**), a bold and complicated structure designed to transfer boats between the Weaver Navigation and the Trent & Mersey. Completed in 1875, it consisted of two iron tanks working up and down inside a large cage of iron tubes and struts. The lift was operated by steam-powered hydraulic rams until 1903, when electrically powered cable pulleys were introduced, altering its silhouette but making it more efficient.

Water supply

Along with the engineering problems of overcoming awkward terrain was the simple prob-lem of supplying a canal with water. Mines, lakes, rivers, streams and springs were all util-ized wherever possible, their water often con-ducted to a canal along narrow feeders and through sluices. Some feeders, like the Welford Arm, Wendover Arm or the River Dee to Trevor section of the Llangollen Canal, were themselves part-navigable. The Wisbech Canal relied on once-a-fortnight spring tides from the River Nene. The tide rose and the canal filled; a strange way of getting water.

The high-ground canals of the Heroic phase were especially vulnerable to water shortages and reservoirs were built to keep their summits topped up. The first large, purpose-built reser-voirs belong to the 1790s and were all con-structed along similar lines. Each consisted of a substantial earth dam, sloped on the outside, puddle-and-masonry lined on the inside. Each had its inflow (from river or stream) controlled by a regulating weir and each had low-level outlets and overflow spillways. The outlets (which were controlled by sluices or valves)

28 *Winterburn Reservoir, Leeds & Liverpool Canal: architecture as scenery. W. Rofe's 'Spanish Steps' water-ladder and low-level outfall culvert.*

connected to the canal either directly via a culvert or indirectly via a feeder channel.

There are early, upland reservoirs at Whaley Bridge on the Peak Forest Canal, at Slaithwaite (with curving earth banks) on the Huddersfield Narrow and at Foulridge on the Leeds & Liverpool. In a lowland setting, Rennie designed Rudyard Reservoir on the Trent & Mersey; Jessop (and Bevan), Marsworth on the Grand Union; and Telford, Belvide and Knighton on the Shropshire Union.

Reservoirs display few architectural features. One exception to this rule is the remote Winterburn Reservoir (28), which feeds the Leeds & Liverpool. The equipment of this 1893 example is splendid. It includes stone wave walls, big iron valve gear and a spectacular water-ladder. The massive, grassy dam has been absorbed into the Dales landscape. A reservoir-keeper's cottage and a rustic stone hut complete the ensemble. Occasionally original valve-houses survive at reservoirs. There is one fine example, a circular plan, iron domed building at Belvide Reservoir (29) and two others, similar but brick-built, at the foot of Rotton Park Reservoir in Birmingham.

The work of controlling water on canals was continuous. Levels had to be maintained, locks bypassed, flood water run off into streams and rivers. Control devices include by-weirs, flood paddles and spillways. By-weirs, consisting of

a small weir and a narrow channel, accompany locks. These brackish, gurgling features, usually brick or stone-lined, can be found on the offside of a lock. Sometimes the weir is culverted beneath a cottage. On the Staffs & Worcester, Brindley designed some circular 'morning glory' lock weirs (30), but their purpose is the same as all the others: to keep water moving and evenly distributed between pounds. Flood paddles (also called hatches or let-offs) often reveal themselves by rusting iron gear set back in the towpath nettles. The paddle opened a brick (or elm) culvert built through the bank and allowed water to escape into a stream or river. Fixed spillways or waste weirs, which are crested apron-like slopes in brick or concrete set at intervals in the canal banks, and more extensive box weirs, running parallel with the bank, served the same purpose.

Few water-control devices were designed to be anything more than functional. Telford's Horseshoe Falls weir on the Llangollen is gracefully curved and scenic, its abstract form typical of larger examples on rivers like the Severn and the Thames. Occasionally, weirs

29 *Valve house, Belvide Reservoir, Shropshire Union Canal: an 1830s design of simple, geometrical shapes. Inside there is a valve which controls the flow of water from the reservoir (behind the concave wall) to the canal feeder.*

were made into a feature. Weaver Navigation sluices of the 1870s are bravely eclectic — engineer's Gothic mixed with sumptuous red and yellow abutments bearing echoes of English Baroque.

Pumping stations

Pumping from rivers, wells, and reservoirs, and back-pumping at lock flights were often essential to water supply. Wind, water and steam were all used to power pumps on canals. Windpumps were probably not common, but were used throughout the Canal Age, from the 1780s on the Oxford to the 1830s, when two were erected to pump water on the Wey

and Arun Junction. They were cheap, low-maintenance structures with a more or less predictable power source. More reliable, but rarer, were waterwheel-driven pumps like that at Melingriffith on the Glamorganshire Canal, or Claverton on the Kennet & Avon, where water is pumped from the River Avon up into the canal. The Claverton pump was designed by Rennie and was working by 1813. It is housed in a simple, T-shaped building made of Bath stone with slate roofs. The wheelhouse is part-weatherboarded. There are no frills. Nor are there any at the former steam-powered pumping station at Widcombe in Bath; just unadorned, square-cut stone and a tapering chimney.

Steam-powered pumping stations were expensive to build and maintain, but in many places they were essential. On the plateau canals of the BCN, with heavy lockage and few reservoirs, 40 engines were at work by 1813,

30 *A 'morning glory' by-weir on the Staffs & Worcester Canal: a late eighteenth century Brindley design, one of a series which included rectangular, oval, and half-moon shapes. The lobster pot trash grill is a later addition* (Derek Pratt, Waterways Photo Library).

31 *Crofton pumping station, Kennet & Avon Canal: engine house with windows, boiler house extension with pitched roof, separate chimney. Reservoir weir equipment in foreground* (BW; Arthur Watts Collection).

pumping water into summit levels. These were either recirculating lock water or were pumping out of mines, and not all were company owned. Georgian pumping stations were plain buildings. That at Crofton (**31**) on the Kennet & Avon houses two steam-powered beam engines which pumped water from a reservoir into the canal. Built in 1809 of brown brick and slate, Crofton's engine house is a three-storey block with regularly spaced windows, in the contemporary tradition of breweries, workhouses and mills, a tradition which still owed much to domestic buildings.

At Tringford on the Wendover Arm a rebuilt station still pumps water into the Grand Union main line. Its rather humdrum external appearance is deceptive. Inside, there is heavy-duty machinery. Below ground level there are Piranesian stairways, narrow corridors, and deep well-shafts. The Tringford Station was part of the complicated arrangements for keeping Tring summit supplied with water. It was supplemented by nine pumps which were installed between Fenny Stratford and Marsworth on the northern approach to the summit. These 'Northern Engines' were for back-pumping: they returned used water to the top of the locks. The whole series was built between

1834–41, the engines housed in brown brick boxes set slap on the canal side. They have hipped roofs but are otherwise utterly plain.

The size and appearance of pumping stations varied. Early examples tended to be more severe-looking and larger than their later replacements, although there are exceptions: the big Brasshouse Lane pumping station, was built in 1892 on a site in Smethwick Cutting which slopes between the old and new Birmingham main lines. It replaced two earlier engines and was large enough to contain two vertical compound engines powering centrifugal pumps which could shift over 5,000,000 gallons of water a day. The engine house is built of alternate courses of hard red and steely blue bricks and has hipped, lantern-lit roofs; machicolated eaves provide some half-starved decoration.

The Victorian urge to put utilitarian structures — railway stations, gasworks, sewage works — into fancy dress affected canals in various ways. One was in the design of new or replacement pumping stations. By the mid nineteenth century ambitious designs were being turned out by company engineers' offices. Some never got off the drawing board and remain anonymous in archive collections; others were built and a few were quite stunning. Leawood pumping station (*c.* 1849) on the Cromford Canal is a fine example; a striking classical design with its engine house, boiler house and tapering chimney strongly emphasized as individual but closely related parts (**32**). The quality of the stonework and its details is excellent and the designer had a rare feel for the dramatic Derwent Valley setting. Braunston pumping station on the Grand Union was built in a freer style (**33**). It replaced an earlier station of 1810 which was similar to Crofton: a solid, three-storey Georgian design, rather spare and domestic-looking, with a fat chimney. The new pumping station was smaller (to contain centrifugal pumps rather than a large beam engine) with round-arched metal windows, some fancy brickwork and a slim chimney

32 *Leawood pumping station, Cromford Canal: a tightly drawn classical design, shoe-horned onto a narrow site beside the canal (*R. Butler*).*

bearing the blue brick inscription GJC (Grand Junction Canal) 1897. Like the old station, the new one pumped water from the Oxford Canal up to one of the Grand Union's summits.

Maintenance yards

Routine maintenance of a canal and its equipment was vital. Most companies owned a maintenance yard, a group of specialized buildings where materials were stored, work-boats serviced and repairs carried out, or new items made such as wooden bridges, lock gates and paddle gearing. On a long canal there were satellite or outpost yards: the main Trent & Mersey yard was at Stone and there were satellites at Etruria and Fradley. The siting of maintenance yards reflected the geography of a canal: there were yards in towns or villages, at junctions, beside lock flights, or at a convenient mid-point along a canal. Outpost yards were usually more isolated and some could only be reached by water or the towpath. The smallest outposts were the canalside huts scattered alongside locks, tunnels and reservoirs. Taken together, these buildings are the physical

33 *Building the second generation Braunston pumping station in the 1890s. Chimney, boiler and pump are in place; brick walls with iron-framed windows are being run up around them (*BW Archives*).*

remains of a pattern of work repeated day-in-day-out on canals and river navigations all over England: the work of gangs going on boats to dredge shallows, patch up bridges, pile banks, repair damaged paddles; the work of carpenters, who made everything from cupboard doors in cottages to boats and lock gates; of blacksmiths who forged ironmongery and made running repairs as necessary; the work of painters, plumbers, bricklayers, fitters, gangers, yardmen, pilemakers, lock-keepers, lengthsmen and general labourers.

Early canal-yard buildings were made of local materials and run up by local builders. On the limestone belt and in northern areas this meant stone walls and stone slates; elsewhere

34 *Hartshill Yard: the multi-purpose maintenance building of c. 1800 which houses a wet dock, blacksmith's shop, carpenter's shop, stores and mess room.* (BW Archives)

it meant brick and plain tiles. Timber-framed sheds, either vertically or horizontally boarded, were common. By the mid-nineteenth century cheap, durable bricks and slate are the most widespread building materials found in maintenance yards. Surfacing usually took the form of cobbles, granite setts or brick pavers with larger open areas a mix of earth and gravel.

On his canal, the Duke of Bridgewater established maintenance and boat-repair facilities at Worsley, right at the heart of his business empire. But there is evidence that other early canal companies let their regular maintenance out to contract, merely supplying and storing materials. This relaxed eighteenth-century approach changed as increased traffic and then railway competition led to a need for better organization. Purpose-built yards with permanent buildings appeared and most of those which survive date from the nineteenth century.

There were many variations in size, layout and buildings. A typical yard might include the following: a dry dock which might be covered or open and which was often at or near the yard's centre; a crane; stables; open sheds; workshops (either separate or multi-purpose); stores or open bunkers for iron, timber, brick, stone, lime, paint; a paddle pit for keeping wooden paddles wet; a pattern shop or loft;

cottages for craftsmen and labourers and per- haps a house for an engineer. Some yards had a steam engine to pump water and run machinery, others had a yard railway to trundle heavy items around.

A close relationship with the canal meant that most yards were either roughly square, linear, or 'off-line' (situated on a short arm off the main line of canal). Sometimes, like boatyards and wharfs — with which they have many similarities — maintenance yards became the focus of a small community, as at Norbury on the Shropshire Union or Hillmorton on the Oxford. This was especially the case where a wharf and a yard shared the same site, like Tardebigge on the Worcester & Birmingham.

The square or rectangular layout was pro- bably the most common, especially for yards designed and built at one go. It was a logical development, best seen at yards like Burscough on the Leeds & Liverpool, Gayton on the Grand Union, Oldbury on the BCN, Ellesmere on the Llangollen and Hartshill on the Coven- try (**34**). Their gates, walls and packed-in buildings express a concern for security and usable space, and create an almost monastic sense of enclosure. Ellesmere Yard (**35**) was built in the Shropshire countryside. Its patchwork of materials, shapes and spaces makes it perhaps the most perfect of all surviving yards: an intriguing jumble of sheds, workshops and cottages, with the former company head office sharing the same site. By contrast, Oldbury Yard stands on a factory-lined loop of the BCN. It began life probably in the 1840s when its covered wet dock and cottage-cum-office were built. In about 1860 a stable block was added and in 1890 a low workshop/stores/office range was built at right angles to the earlier buildings: Oldbury grew organically according to com- pany needs. Today its dour brick buildings are hemmed between the giant head-bank of Rotton Park Reservoir and shabby industrial premises. It is a grim urban site.

Linear layouts are found at yards like Sneyd on the Wyrley & Essington, Norbury on the

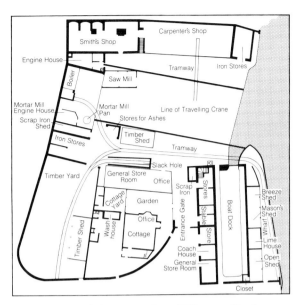

35 *Early twentieth-century plan of Ellesmere Yard, Llangollen Canal: a compact, square layout, enclosing walls and an open waterside (*P. Dunn*).*

Shropshire Union, and the later yards of Hatton and Bulbourne on the Grand Union. The last two have impressive ranges of buildings. Hatton's staggered, gabled workshops and signal-box-like office form stern silhouettes at the top of the great lock flight. Bulbourne's workshops, all built by the Grand Junction Canal Co. in the 1890s, are unmatched for completeness (**36**). Here there are two lines of stores and workshops clustered between a manager's house and a row of cottages.

Off-line maintenance yards are rare. Hill- morton is the best example; a secretive site tucked away behind a bridge on a quiet arm of water. A map of 1793 shows no buildings at all at 'Hill Morton'. Neither does an OS 'Survey Drawing' of 1813. But the OS one-inch map of 1834 shows signs of activity and several build- ings are clearly marked on a local map of *c.* 1840. Hillmorton Yard was established in the wake of the great northern Oxford improve- ments of the 1830s (see **4**).

There was a great deal of variety in indi- vidual buildings from one maintenance yard to the next. Dry docks refer to the job they do by

36 *Bulbourne Yard, Grand Union Canal: an eclectically detailed tower adds an exuberant note to ranges of well-lit stock brick and slate workshops (*Derek Pratt, Waterways Photo Library*)*

their clear relationship with boats and water. Sometimes they are open, sometimes covered, or fully enclosed, when their sparse appearance, low roofline and the size and shape of their doorways explain their purpose. Workshops are usually identifiable by their large windows and large sliding or plank doors. Their interiors are spartan: open roof trusses, often of the industrial king-post type; brick or wooden block floors; panelled offices and lean-tos. Those still in use are cluttered with lockers, butch-looking work benches and grimy tools. Some workshops have a uniform, factory-like appearance. Others resemble agricultural buildings: plain brick sheds with pitched roofs, their austerity

relieved only by simple details — a rounded corner, dentilled eaves, diamond-pattern ventilation holes. There was rarely any conscious attempt at 'design'. One of the most important buildings in a yard was the blacksmith's shop; where this was separate it was usually a small symmetrical building with a central door flanked by windows. Inside was a forge built of brick with a hood chimney. This was the blacksmith's private realm; a jungle of old iron, hung up in sheaves, piled against walls, strewn around anvils and benches. There were bellows to blow on the fire with, and a water trough close by, with tongs leaning against it. Here, wrought-iron bars were heated, twisted and cut like toffee to make hundreds of small items of canal ironmongery. Here cogs, collars, and pins were made from wooden casts pressed into trays of sand.

Multi-purpose buildings are an important

maintenance yard type. These contained perhaps a small dock, a blacksmith's and a carpenter's shop (sometimes a sawpit), and offices stores and lofts, all under one roof. There is one at Norbury and a much smaller one at Lapworth on the Stratford-on-Avon; the best example is at Hartshill Yard, established in the 1790s on the Coventry. The spatial organization of this building is fascinating. It is still used, and its cramped stores-loft is an Aladdin's Cave: the walls and floor are lined with racks and sacks of rose-headed and cut canal nails, collars, cotters, coach bolts, pulleys, pins, cups, staples, washers, catches, paddle racks, pinions, large and small rollers, cogs, pig rings, stop plank handles, spades, rakes and old scythes.

Strung out at intervals along a canal were smaller maintenance outposts; jumbled buildings at the end of a dusty track, often consisting of no more than a blacksmith-cum-carpenter's shop, some open sheds and a stable. Day-to-day work tools and materials would be kept in these places: stop planks, bits of timber, ropes, a handturned grindstone, hayforks and scythes for mowing the towpath, billhooks and axes for hedge cutting. A craftsman who was an all-rounder, who could do some woodwork and smithing, would be based here with a couple of lengthsmen. Two former outposts on the

Oxford Canal are those at Claydon (**37**), a tight, wedge-shaped site next to a lock, and Napton where three men ('Uncle' Thorneycroft, 'Ginger' Taylor and 'Wink' Lines) were employed in the 1950s. Together they kept Napton Locks and a long section of the Oxford summit maintained.

Lengthsmen (a 'length' varied; in some places it meant the distance between two bridges, in others an eight-mile stretch of canal) were in the frontline of canal maintenance. Traditionally each man devoted his entire working life to looking after his length. He often lived in a cottage on the canal bank or at the back of a canal yard. A lengthsman walked the towpath regularly, keeping culverts cleared, banks mended, and the water free of rubbish and fallen boughs. In summer he mowed the greensward. In winter he went hedge-laying and hedge clearing, lighting warming fires along the towpath to burn sticks, weeds and trimmings. When out on a lonely stretch, a lengthman kept his tools in a wooden cabin on a work boat or 'flat' or in a small canalside hut. The

37 *Oxford Canal outpost at Claydon: a huddle of shuttered workshops, stores and stabling forming an intimate lockside site (*BW; Arthur Watts Collection*).*

work was invigorating but repetitive: for some it meant 40 or 50 years spent trudging up and down the same few miles. And although a lengthsman knew and loved every foot of his own patch, beyond that he knew nothing: other parts of the canal remained as mysterious as Timbuktu.

Trim

Humblest of all canal equipment is the trim, which means all those accessories that once made a canal legal and workable: mile posts, bridge and lock numberplates, company boundary markers, loading plates, warning notices, bollards, dollies and cleats.

Canal acts required mileposts to be fixed on banks to regulate 'distances and tonnage', so that tolls could be calculated. Eighteenth-century mileposts were of wood or stone and those that survive are often weathered and worn, their inscriptions defaced or barely legible. Examples can be found mouldering in the undergrowth along the Oxford and on the green edges of the Selby Canal. The Peak Forest Canal has a 1790s series of tombstone-shaped mileposts. The Macclesfield has a collection dating from the 1820s. By the early nineteenth century cast-iron mileposts became common (**38a** and **b**) and good ones survive on the Trent & Mersey. There are similar examples on the Shropshire Union, dating from the 1820s and probably designed by Telford. This type consists of a foundry-cast round-topped post with bulging plates inscribed with place-names and distances in sturdy English clarendons. The bleak banks of the Gloucester & Sharpness have a series of angle-faced mileposts, again dating from the early nineteenth century, with classical lettering with thick-and-thin strokes. The 1890s re-shaping of the Grand Union included a painstaking survey by the meticulous Thomas Millner and resulted in the replacement of a scrambled collection of wood and stone mileposts with a uniform series of cast-iron plates, including small intermediate plates for quarter, half and three-quarter miles.

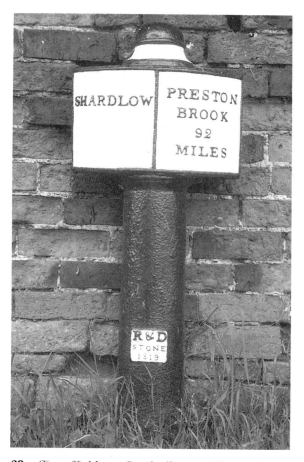

38a *Trent & Mersey Canal milepost, 1819, cast-iron.*

The Leicester Line was re-numbered at the same time; hitherto, distances were splendidly marked by elms and poplars at mile and half-mile intervals. All the Grand Union plates are oblong with sans-serif inscriptions, and have much in common with the wholesome style of Victorian railways.

Canal-owning railway companies often put up loading plates at bridges. Oblong or square notices were fixed to the roadside parapets, and lozenge-shaped signs were erected on steel rails at bridge approaches. These plates were cast iron with close lettering, painted white on a black background, some of it on removable panels for varying restrictions. The Great Western Railway scattered them all over the canals which became part of its vast empire. Canal companies put up similar signs and, like the railways, they drove boundary posts into the ground to mark the extent of their ownership. Flat oval plates inscribed MR denote Midland Railway territory on the Ashby Canal and on the Kennet & Avon round drums — like biscuit tins — mounted on broad-gauge rail were hammered into place by the GWR. These bear early twentieth-century dates. On the Shropshire Union, Grand Union and BCN plain phalluses stamped GJCC, SUC or BCN can be found here and there. Most surviving boundary posts are made of cast iron. Others were stone or concrete. Occasionally, boundary plates were set into an urban towpath. The most insignificant (in one sense) items of waterway trim are the numberplates attached to buildings and structures. In the eighteenth century, numbers were often carved into keystones on bridges. Later, cast-iron plates became more usual. BCN bridges have cast name plates, with appropriately utilitarian and thin lettering.

Bollards and ring cleats are probably the most commonly found objects on the waterways. They occur especially at locksides, landings and once-busy wharfs and basins. Ring cleats (or mooring rings) made of wrought iron and set into wooden jettying or masonry coping fulfil a similar function to bollards and are a tiny but essential waterway detail. Bollards come in many shapes and sizes, ranging from the humble dolly (a small bollard for tying up narrow boats) to larger dolphins, bulbs and mooring posts. Like notes in a musical score,

dozens dot the banks of the Gloucester & Sharpness ship canal. Bollards vary in appearance. There are square blocks, asymmetrical shapes, mushrooms and upside-down cones. Most are of iron, stone or concrete, usually painted white, or with virile black and white stripes to make them visible at night. At some locks, hardwood strapping stumps survive in a state of pleasing decay. Designed to do a simple job — to slow boats down with a rope deftly flung around them — they have twisted and rotted into a 'poor man's sculpture' of weird cracks and surfaces.

38b *Grand Union Canal (Welford Arm) milepost, 1893, cast-iron (*BW; Arthur Watts Collection*).*

3

Bridges, aqueducts and tunnels

A bridge rising above a cornfield, an aqueduct ennobling a slice of rolling countryside, a tunnel yawning darkly at the end of a deep cutting: these are powerful, architectural images of the Canal Age. Bridges, aqueducts and tunnels were expensive to build and maintain, but they were a vital part of canal construction, solving the problem of taking roads and tracks across canals and of taking canals over valleys and through hillsides. Working structures ranging from coarse Pioneering bridges to grand Heroic aqueducts left new formations in the landscape. Made from simple materials — brick, stone, timber, iron — the best of these structures reveal something of the energy and imagination of their engineers.

Standard bridges

An Oxford Canal 'chain book' lists, in July 1840, the following types of bridges: 'Towing Path Bridge, Occupation [accommodation] Bridge, Turnpike Road Bridge, Drawbridge, Parish Road Bridge'. These bridges all had the same function — to allow canal and land traffic to across one another's path without hindrance — but they were of different types and materials. The chain book summarizes them as '155 Brick Bridges of various kinds, 22 Stone Bridges, 10 Archways of various kinds, 42 Drawbridges, 7 Cast Iron Tow Path Bridges, 4 Wooden Tow Path Bridges, 5 Foot Bridges (Wood)'. Most of these bridges were the humped, narrow-waisted accommodation type,

which is the commonest architectural form found on canals. So common, in fact, that in the Heroic phase it became a standard design; the same thing out of different hands. Thousands were built during the Canal Age. Rees's *Cyclopaedia* (1819) confidently illustrates a typical example. It is one that will stand for all.

Brindley and his followers built the first brick and stone canal bridges. On the Bridgewater and the old Chester Canal (now part of the Shropshire Union), on the Trent & Mersey (**39**) and Staffs & Worcester, brick bridges were built, some with a crude, homely charm, others with the graceful, flowing lines of eighteenth-century England. With a few curious excep-

39 *Pioneering lock tail bridge at Colwich on the Trent & Mersey Canal: rustic functionalism of the early 1770s.*

tions, notably on the Staffs & Worcester, these Pioneering bridges are of two kinds: bridges with arches spanning both canal and towpath, and bridges which are built across lock tails, with a narrow arch across the canal only. The latter cleverly utilized the fall of ground and avoided the need for steep approach ramps on the roadway. Both kinds of bridge, with slight variations, became part of the architectural programme of most later canals, even those which also made use of timber bridges.

A typical Pioneering brick accommodation bridge was curved both in plan and elevation, giving it great strength and a solid appearance. Often there was a stone band or label around the arch; an eighteenth-century detail which occurs around window or door openings. Stone copings were squared off or rounded, and flush with the brickwork. These prototype bridges were perfectly fit for their purpose. The Heroic phase merely altered the details, each engineer producing designs which local contractors could build. Designs drawn by Jessop, Rennie and Telford showing plans and perspective views are strikingly similar, whether in brick or stone. In each case the basic geometry and form reveal the function and all mix economy with strength. Their foundations rest on boulder clay or on wooden piers. Their walls are battered (i.e. backwards-leaning) and splay outwards to ease the passage of cattle or swaying farm carts. They have a string course running across at parapet level and their copings are rounded to throw off rain and prevent traffic catching at edges. Arches are often protected by curved iron rubbing strakes; bold black ones with wavy flanges on the Shropshire Union. Brindley had used timber fenders. Wooden rollers, bull-nosed engineering bricks or free-standing iron posts served the same purpose.

The standard design works equally well in brick or stone (**40**). There are honey-coloured examples on the Kennet & Avon and Oxford where they run across the great limestone belt. In the north, the Leeds & Liverpool, Lancaster, Peak Forest, Rochdale and Macclesfield all

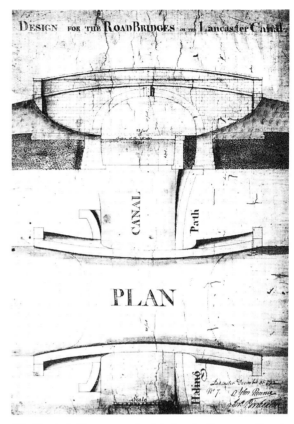

40 *Heroic bridge: a standard design for Lancaster Canal bridges, dated 1792 and signed by John Rennie and his contractor J. Pinkerton (*BW Archives*).*

have stone bridges of high quality. There are hundreds of brick accommodation bridges scattered across the Midlands, ranging in colour from orange to deep plum. Sometimes the names of the building contractors are known. On the Lancaster, to begin with, Rennie relied on the Pinkertons to carry out his designs. On the Oxford, Hollingsworth and Coates built stone bridges for £50 each, supplying all their materials except lime. They used stone from Heyford Quarry. Another contractor, Stanfield, used Atterbury stone for bridge building on the Oxford. Despite the adoption of an almost universal appearance, building the bridges was still an intensely local affair. This accounts for the rich diversity of textures and details; the subtle colour changes between the brickwork of two neighbouring bridges, or the use of 'best burnt' headers around an arch ring. Stone bridges on the Lancaster Canal are of two main types; smooth-ashlared with rounded parapets and rock-faced with parapets which rise to a point. Both types have walls which curl and curve, sometimes one way, sometimes another. Occasionally cryptic masons' marks can be found. Close scrutiny of copings is especially rewarding; on Trent & Mersey bridges the dusky-pink sandstones are finished with a variety of herringbone, linenfold, dashed, speckled and pock-marked tooling.

Tail, roving, and skew bridges

Not all bridges followed the orderly rhythms of the standard design. Lock and bridge combinations vary from Brindley's rustic Pioneering types to complex combinations of lock walls, bridge walls, steps and ramps, all modelled in brick or stone and fitting together in fascinating ways. Benjamin Outram's tightly designed Marple Locks, on the Peak Forest, emphasizes the tectonic intimacy of such combinations.

41 *Fluid stonework on the Macclesfield Canal; a turnover bridge of the late 1820s with a horse ramp spiralling between wings that gracefully curl back on themselves* (BW; Arthur Watts Collection).

Here, lock chambers and tail bridges have ceased to be separate components; they are welded together. This is no-nonsense, millstone grit work of 1803–05, built to do a job and last. Roving and turnover bridges (where a towpath changes sides) display similar skill in the modelling of brick or stonework. The roving bridge at Great Haywood is a famous eighteenth-century example of mobile, snaking lines. A smooth-faced, 1830s stone bridge rolls its way across the Shropshire Union's Newport Branch at Norbury. This is one of the type boatmen nicknamed 'rainbow bridges' because of their pleasing symmetry. Some bridges are complicated by separate roadways and walled towpath approaches. On the Macclesfield Canal there are shy-looking turnover bridges with high parapets and winding ramps which curl back on themselves (**41**). The contrast of the rugged stone and the plastic shapes into which it is bent is visually satisfying. These specialized structures came alive when a nodding horse trailing a rope went up, across, and beneath them.

There are certain places where a slightly different kind of bridge was called for: where a road crossed a canal at an angle a skew bridge was built to keep the road straight. Skew

bridges were not uncommon on canals and appear to have been a Pioneering achievement. William Yates' map of Warwickshire (1793) shows a number of road bridges crossing the Coventry and the Birmingham & Fazeley at unmistakably skewed angles. These were original bridges built in the 1770s and 1780s. Survivals on the ground are rarer, although there are two (one of them rebuilt) at Amington on the Coventry. Early skew bridges like these were built with offset courses of bricks in their arches, a clumsy but effective arrangement. Later bridges, like that at Great Bedwyn on the Kennet & Avon, show winding courses coming into use, although there is evidence that the bricklayers here struggled with Rennie's specification. Stone seems to have been handled more confidently than brick in skew construction. March Barn Bridge on the Rochdale, completed *c.* 1800, is an early example, possibly designed by Jessop and clearly built by a highly skilled mason. Later stone examples on the Macclesfield are outstanding: in sunlight and shadow their winding courses look carved rather than fitted together stone by stone.

Brick and stone bridges which were special for social rather than technological reasons were ornamental or 'fancy' bridges. Here and there canals passed through the parks and estates of the landed gentry. The landowners often insisted upon, or were sweetened by the promise of, a bridge that would embellish their property. Usually a classical design was required, along the lines of Lady's Bridge on the Kennet & Avon, Avenue Bridge on the Shropshire Union, or Cassiobury Park Bridge on the Grand Union. Solomon's Bridge (**42**), on the Grand Union, is a rare example of Regency Gothic.

Wooden fixed, swing and lift-bridges

Wood was part of the texture of eighteenth- and nineteenth-century canals. It was cheaply available and easily fabricated by common-place skills into a range of useful accessories. Fixed wooden footbridges, typically supported

42 *Solomon's Bridge, Grand Union Canal: a Regency Gothic 'fancy' bridge, built in the late 1790s to appease a local landowner (*BW; Arthur Watts Collection*).*

on brick piers with wooden steps and a flat deck, are found on canals and on navigations and are now invariably recent in date. A curious nineteenth-century example is that at Drayton Manor on the Birmingham & Fazeley, which boasts two castellated stair turrets with a narrow, overhead deck slung between them. Even narrower are the occasional bridges which consist merely of wooden trestles carrying a single beam with canted-out handrails attached. Elementary footbridges occur at locks such as Foxton or Bingley Five Rise, where a pleasing utility is achieved by planks, rails and white paint.

Wooden bridges that swung aside, or were raised or drawn back, were another way of crossing a canal or a river navigation. They were especially useful on the low-lying water-ways which fed into the Humber and were often opened by the wives of lengthsmen, who expected to be tipped for this work. Swing bridges were easy and cheap to make but required regular maintenance. Rees's *Cyclopaedia* describes a 'flat platform of wood strongly framed together, covered with planks, and having side rails . . .'. Examples on the Kennet & Avon and on the Leeds & Liverpool retain the form of the originals. Rennie's drawings for swing-bridges on the Kennet & Avon show simple plank decks and handrails, mounted on

43 *A wooden skew lift-bridge (a very rare type) on the Prees Branch of the Llangollen Canal. The design dates from the 1790s. The bridge is raised by pulling on the chain hanging from the counterweighted box (*BW; Arthur Watts Collection*).*

a sub-frame that turned on a ball-race, a system which became common in the nineteenth century and which was used on Jessop's giant wooden swing-bridge over the Ouse at Selby. Double-leaved swing-bridges, with clean, elegant lines, were built on the Caledonian and on the Gloucester & Sharpness in the 1820s (see **5**). Canals and river navigations sometimes have swing-bridges across their locks, like those at Naburn on the Ouse. Foot swing-bridges were once common in yards and docks. Smallest of all were the plankways which swung on a pivot and joined BCN toll-offices with the canal banks. These were worked by means of a lever. Most swing-bridges were pulled open with a chain, pushed open by a wooden beam or else opened and closed by means of a winch and chain.

Lift-bridges are now increasingly rare. The southern Oxford has a series of a unique type with plank decks and raking balance beams, mounted on brick abutments. A handful of 'Dutch' or overhead frame lift-bridges survive on the Llangollen (**43**) and in slightly different form on the Northampton Arm. There are a few Scottish examples (called bascules) on the Forth & Clyde. Impressive, double-leaved examples appear in engineers' notebooks and contract drawings. There were unusual iron lift

and draw-back bridges in dock and factory areas (**44**). Most of these can now be traced only in old photographs. On the Crinan Canal, a draw-back or roller bridge remains in use at Dunardry.

Iron bridges

New materials and technology meant new types of bridges on canals. Rees's *Cyclopaedia* tells us that it was the 'ingenuity and enterprise of British artists' that gave rise, to the introduction, from the 1790s onwards, of cast-iron bridges. Two early examples, both of 1800, span the Kennet & Avon in the lovely Sydney Gardens length in Bath. There is evidence that at least one of them was designed by Rennie. Each is decorated and different from the other, but both are constructed of cast iron ribs, with cast-iron deck plates made at Ironbridge by the Coalbrookdale Company. Macclesfield Bridge (1815–16) is a heavier-looking ornamental bridge carrying a park road across the Regent's Canal. It consists of ten Greek Doric columns supporting a brick

44 *Turn Bridge, Huddersfield Broad Canal: a hand-cranked lift-bridge of 1865. Originally the framework was of wood, giving the bridge an appearance of appropriate solidity (*BW; Arthur Watts Collection*).*

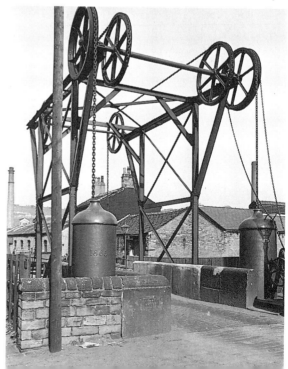

52

45 *Late phase prefabricated iron bridges at Windmill End Junction on the BCN. The engine house (c. 1831) is typical of many that once pumped water from mines into Black Country canals (Derek Pratt, Waterways Photo Library).*

arch. It was designed, with an eye on the current Greek Revival fashion, by James Morgan. When a gunpowder barge blew up beneath it in 1874 the iron columns survived intact and the bridge was rebuilt.

The impact of iron on canals was felt most of all on the BCN, where between *c.* 1800 and 1820 there was much replacement of older wooden bridges. The new structural forms — cast-iron arches and beams — were mass-produced by the flourishing canalside foundries of the Black Country. Bridges could now be prefabricated, boated up to prepared sites and simply fitted together. Iron bridges are a hallmark of Midlands canals of the 1830s and 1840s. Many were built by Horseley Iron Works of Tipton, whose name and often the date are cast in raised letters on the arch ring (see **6**). These thinly stretched webs of iron are typical of canals like the Dudley, Walsall, Titford, Gower and Tame Valley. Often they are towpath bridges over factory arms and basin entrances. The most memorable are the roving bridges at junctions; lithe cambered silhouettes with parapet patterns as sharp as cut paper. These patterns usually take the form of Saltire crosses, sometimes with a run of Gothic quatrefoils or brattishing across the top, just below the handrail. Abutments and wing walls are of Staffordshire blue or grey-brindled engineering brick, with stone caps and corners. Functional and hard-wearing, these bridges were designed for maximum use. Their stonework and handrails are scored and cleft by the razing of countless tow-ropes. Now they swoop eerily across once-busy junctions or provide the sole focus of abandoned industrial sites (**45**).

The BCN and Horseley bridges came as a kit consisting of deck plates with flanged sides, handrails and beams; these components were held together with bolts. A slightly earlier development involving smaller precast units was that of the split bridge. Split bridges consist of two short iron decks, cantilevered out from

46 *A split bridge on the south Stratford-on-Avon Canal: one of a series of cheap bridges built between 1812–16.*

brick abutments, leaving a gap or split between them to allow tow ropes to slip through. At one go these simple bridges did away with the need for expensive arched bridges with towpaths underneath. But they were only suitable for accommodation purposes, taking loads of no more than a ton, and occur only on a few Midlands canals which were built on the cheap: William Whitmore's south Stratford-on-Avon constructed in 1812–16 on a mean budget, has the best collection (**46**). Similar to split bridges but smaller still are the giddy-making footplates cantilevered out from the tail walls of locks. These come in two halves or else are mounted like a springboard, with a gap left under one end for ropes to slide beneath. There are cast-iron examples with ring pattern brackets on the Staffs & Worcester and on the Trent & Mersey, although these are not contemporary with the original construction.

At the other end of the scale are big iron and steel bridges. Telford's Smethwick Cutting of 1827–9 is crossed by what the *British Almanac* of 1830 described as 'the largest canal bridge in the world; it is made of iron: the arch is one hundred and fifty feet span, and over it passes a public roadway twenty-six feet wide'. Galton was a real *tour de force*: a ribbed, cast-iron arch bridge, with brick and dressed stone abutments — a splendid advertisement for the Birmingham New Main Line. E. Leader

Williams designed some massive iron swing-bridges for the Weaver Navigation and the Manchester Ship Canal. Hayhurst Bridge, an electric-powered example of 1900 on the Weaver in Northwich, has a deck which turns on a roller race supported on floating pontoons. Thin iron railings and deck gates with filigree lamp brackets form a sharp contrast to its huge bracing and undercarriage girders. At one end is a black-and-white wooden control cabin. The bridge is still in daily use for road traffic.

Concrete bridges

Concrete bridges belong largely to the twentieth century. Among the handful of early examples are a bridge in London which carried a tramway across the Regent's Canal, a towpath bridge on the Trent in Newark, and one or two minor road bridges across the navigable fen drains of Lincolnshire. The Grand Union modernization of the 1930s produced a number of reinforced concrete 'slab and tee-beam portal' bridges, where the slab or deck was covered with asphalt and tarmacadam and the parapets had cast patterns recalling BCN iron bridges of 100 years earlier. Examples at Stockton and Hatton are surprisingly slim-looking. Other 1930s road bridges, usually built as part of a widening scheme, are often lumpen and grit-faced, with vague Mexican details or the highway authority's initials and a date cast into the parapet. Mid- to late-twentieth century road and motorway bridges are occasionally light, well-designed structures, but most have unforgiving details and chilly undersides of slowly dirtying concrete.

Brick and stone aqueducts

The largest and most spectacular canal structures are aqueducts which crossed rivers, streams, roads and later railways. They were expensive to build but they kept a canal level, thereby saving water and avoiding the need for locks. Some aqueducts are plain and anonymous; others are grand architectural statements which exploit the natural drama of their setting.

The Duke of Bridgewater, inspired no doubt by Grand Tour memories of Roman remains and French canals, conceived the idea of keeping his canal level above the valley of the Irwell by taking it across on an aqueduct. His success seized the imagination. Contemporary prints show boats crossing one another at different levels: a 'wonder and delight' to visitors. Barton Aqueduct opened in 1761 and appears to have been as much the work of the Duke and his gifted agent John Gilbert as of Brindley. It was of stone and consisted of three segmental arches with cutwater piers. It had no parapets, as is typical of early aqueducts, and it was large by Pioneering standards. The aqueducts which followed, designed by Brindley and his followers, were less exciting.

Three similar examples all completed between 1766 and 1771 illustrate the Brindley type. Rugeley Aqueduct on the Trent & Mersey is of brick; Great Haywood Aqueduct and Milford Aqueduct (47), both on the Staffs & Worcester, are shorter and stone-faced. All three are low-lying, low-level structures. Each consists of a row of squat arches carrying very thick and wide rubble-and-puddle walls within which the canal is contained in a trough. In each case the trough is as narrow as possible. Beneath each aqueduct the river has been artificially widened so as to slacken its flow between the obstructing piers. The widenings are visible today. These three aqueducts are really oversized culverts. They have no height because no height was required and they amble across their rivers without taking any risks.

Heroic canals demanded more daring engineering. This, and the Romantic conception that an aqueduct might be a sublime object in the landscape, produced some spectacular examples, firstly in stone and then in cast iron. Robert Whitworth's Kelvin Aqueduct, built in the 1780s on the Forth & Clyde, was one of the earliest big expensive stone aqueducts.

47 Milford Aqueduct, Staffs & Worcester Canal: a coarse, Pioneering four-arched structure, designed by Brindley and built by Thomas Dadford the elder in the 1770s (BW; Arthur Watts Collection).

48 *Lune Aqueduct, Lancaster Canal: a gritty splendidly-scaled classical design. This is Rennie's Heroic masterpiece (*RCHME Crown Copyright*).*

Designed as a piece of architecture, it has boldly rusticated arches, sharp cutwaters and curving upper walls. It inspired John Rennie, whose classical stone aqueducts of the 1790s are heroic in every sense of the word.

Approaching Bath on the Kennet & Avon there is a sequence of Rennie aqueducts: Biss, Semington, Avoncliff, Dundas — the effect is cumulative. Biss and Semington are minor aqueducts but Rennie took care to get them looking right, providing meticulous drawings of cornice and parapet details. Avoncliff is grander, with three arches, blockily rusticated piers and ashlared stonework. Dundas is the crescendo: tons of Bath stone hung triumphantly above the fast-flowing Avon, modelled with a dignity and scale that is truly Roman (see **7**). One of Rennie's drawings reveals the skeleton beneath: the central arch and flanking oval flood arches, the heavy-duty foundations, the puddle-lined trough and iron tie-bars; internal reinforcements taking the strain of lateral pressure. An accompanying elevation shows the suave classical skin, notable for its use of paired pilasters, massive entablature and jutting cornices. On bright days Dundas is cast into a most magnificent effect of *gravitas*.

Up north on the Lancaster, Rennie designed the even bigger Lune Aqueduct (**48**), 600ft (183m) long and 62ft (19m) high. It has five semicircular arches, rusticated piers, pilasters with a downward batter and curving wing walls. Among masonry aqueducts, Lune's splendour remains unsurpassed.

Not all aqueducts stood up as well as Rennie's. On the Cromford, Jessop's Bullbridge Aqueduct failed in 1792 and when his Wigwell Aqueduct on the same canal cracked in 1793 he rebuilt it at his own expense. In 1808 Jessop's Wolverton Aqueduct on the Grand Union collapsed and was replaced by an iron trough aqueduct. Outram had more success with his aqueducts on the Peak Forest Canal of the 1790s. His River Tame Aqueduct, cramped close to the junction with the Ashton Canal, recalls earlier Pioneering examples with its solid, unadorned stonework and chunky details.

Outram's Marple Aqueduct, of the same date, forms a Heroic contrast. Its three tall arches, with spandrels pierced by bullseyes (to lighten the structure), are simple but effective.

Other brick and stone aqueducts include later canal flyovers like Steward Aqueduct, which takes the BCN Old Main Line across the New Main Line. This is a twin-arched structure of brick with stone dressings. Cast-iron parapet rails with intersecting heads form its one concession to decoration. Another example, Hazelhurst Aqueduct, takes the Leek Branch across its parent Caldon Canal by means of a robust brick structure dated 1841. There are single-arch stone aqueducts of distinction on the Lancaster and Macclesfield canals. Elsewhere there are culvert-type aqueducts or underbridges which allow roads and tracks to cross through large embankments. Two underbridges punch through Weedon embankment on the Grand Union, and Shelmore Great Bank on the Shropshire Union has two barrel-vaulted examples in smooth finished sandstone. There are others on canals such as the Bridgewater, the Llangollen, the Macclesfield and the remodelled northern stretches of the Oxford.

Brick or stone aqueducts were costly and time-consuming to build. They were also limited by technical considerations of height, length and weight. One solution was to introduce new materials and design a new kind of structure: the iron trough aqueduct.

Iron aqueducts
The advantages of iron aqueducts were that they could be cast in prefabricated parts, did not require tons of supporting masonry and were relatively easy to maintain. Iron could span depths and distances that were unthinkable in stone; its only long-term weakness was that it would eventually rust. The mid-1790s saw intense interest in the potential of structural ironwork, and development of the new material led quickly to the design and construction of prototype aqueducts.

In 1796 the versatile Outram introduced a small iron aqueduct on his Derby Canal. That has been demolished, but a large and very important one completed in the same year on the Shrewsbury Canal at Longdon-on-Tern still exists (**49**). Longdon which replaced an unsuitable stone aqueduct, was designed by Reynolds (the Shropshire ironmaster) and Telford. They worked together on the project and although the result was innovatory and long-lasting, it owed much to the work of contemporaries, such as Watkin George's Pontcafnau ('bridge of troughs'), a combined tramroad and water-power aqueduct which was built at Merthyr Tydfil in 1793. Longdon is a primitive, clumsy affair with interesting details. It consists of a framework of iron girders and three groups of supporting iron legs carrying a trough of bolted-together iron plates with an iron towpath running alongside. The whole thing was reputedly made watertight by packing its joints with a super-glue made of flannel and boiled sugar.

In the same exhilarating years of the 1790s Telford and Jessop were discussing ways of

49 *Longdon-on-Tern Aqueduct, Shrewsbury Canal. According to Telford it was 'made all of cast-iron, excepting only the nuts and screws, which are of wrought iron'. Crudely detailed but boldly conceived — a prototype for Pontcysyllte (*RCHME Crown Copyright*).*

taking the Llangollen Canal across the valleys of the Dee and Ceiriog on the Welsh border. Two aqueducts were needed and Jessop recommended 'an Iron Aqueduct' for both. For the Ceiriog crossing at Chirk, iron was rejected and instead a compromise was built: a ten-arch stone aqueduct with a trough bed of bolted cast-iron plates, which reduced the weight on the aqueduct's foundations and tied its walls together at the same time. Chirk was built between 1796 and 1801 and is a handsome, unadorned structure that prefigures much straightforward railway building which followed. It is a major work and a striking object in the landscape. The tourist Sir Richard Colt Hoare found that the 'soft mellow yellow tint of the stone' looked beautiful in 'picturesque light', and the watercolourist Cotman was moved to paint it. But Chirk was overshadowed by its great neighbour, the iron aqueduct Pontcysyllte.

50 *Pontcysyllte Aqueduct: austere beauty out of technical problems overcome. Height, length, and space revealed between the piers create real visual excitement. This was the most Heroic structure built on Britain's industrial canals (*BW Archives*).*

Pontcysyllte is an icon of the Industrial Revolution (**50**). Rees's *Cyclopaedia* attributes it simply to 'Mr Jessop', but it seems to have been a collaborative effort between Jessop, Telford, the mason John Simpson, and the iron-master William Hazeldine. From a practical point of view it owed much to Longdon-on-Tern. Pontcysyllte was built across the Dee valley between 1795 and 1805, with a slight pause to allow Chirk to be completed first. The aqueduct is a cast-iron trough consisting of precast flanged and bolted iron plates. Unlike Longdon, its towpath is ingeniously cantilevered across the trough, allowing water to move freely beneath. Seventeen tapering stone piers support the trough.

Each span is carried on four iron arch-ribs, the outer ones bolted together to emulate the form of a segmental stone arch. The qualities and strengths of cast iron were as yet imperfectly understood and engineers could only fall back for certain structural details on masonry and carpentry techniques. And where traditional skills were called for at Pontcysyllte — for the curving stone abutments and slender stone piers — the craftsmanship is excellent. The

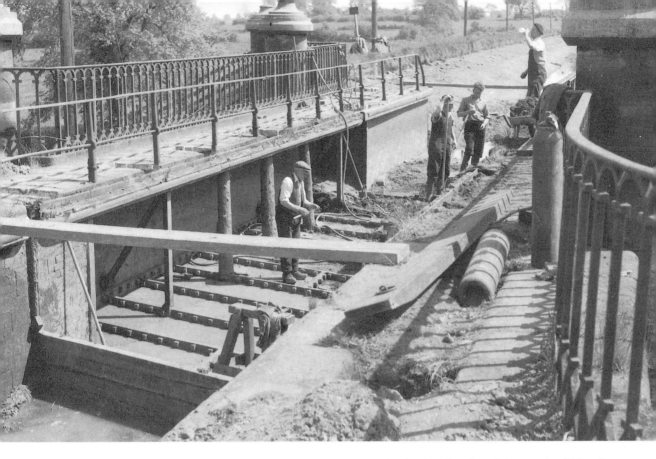

piers are partly hollow (Jessop's idea), which made their actual building easier, lessened the weight on the foundations and made subsequent inspection less of a problem. After its completion Pontcysyllte stood full of water for six months, until it was clear that winter ice and summer heat left its two-inch thick plates unaffected.

Pontcysyllte was immediately hailed as a masterpiece. Artists painted and engraved it. Fashionable people went to gawp at it. Sir Walter Scott said it was 'the most impressive work of art he had ever seen' and a French engineer, visiting the 'sky-born canal' in 1816, found it 'enclosed in its iron envelope, hung, like something enchanted, on its high, slender pillars, a supreme work of architecture...'. The success of Pontcysyllte went to Telford's head. Its inclusion in the *Atlas to the Life of Thomas Telford*, implying that he alone was its creator, was a powerful piece of myth-making.

Nothing approaching the scale or the austere beauty of Pontcysyllte was achieved again but the use and development of cast-iron aqueducts continued into the early nineteenth century. Wolverton Aqueduct, a double-span trough on the Grand Union, was built in 1811. Its engineer Benjamin Bevan went and sought inspiration from Longdon, Chirk and Pontcysyllte and he got Reynolds to supply the iron trough which has 'voussoir'-type plates similar to those on Pontcysyllte. A minor detail of this aqueduct is the existence of small cattle creeps running through its embankment at either end. In 1813 William Whitmore completed two iron-trough aqueducts on the south Stratford-on-Avon Canal: Edstone, which at 520ft (158m) is the second longest after Pontcysyllte, and Wootton Wawen, which is similar but shorter. Edstone is carried across a shallow valley on plain brick piers. Its plates are bolted in the usual way but

52 *Greek severity pierced by a rainbow: an iron trough hung from two iron arches. George Leather's unique and striking Stanley Ferry Aqueduct (*BW Archives*).*

have straight edges, and the whole trough is supported by huge pierced iron beams, a significant departure from the established practice of using arched iron ribs. The towpath is slung alongside the trough in the Longdon manner. Wootton Wawen was a similar design, although its plates are of unequal length. It bears an oval plaque dated 1813. Further down the canal another, smaller, aqueduct bears the Horseley name and the date 1834. This replaced an original aqueduct which failed, and is a miniature version of Whitmore's larger two.

Engine Arm Aqueduct on a branch of the BCN Old Main Line was designed by Telford in *c.* 1828 and provides a rare example of a canal aqueduct displaying decorative as well as structural cast iron: there is Gothic tracery along the fascia below the trough. And on the Shropshire Union, Telford created a modestly decorated aqueduct type which spawned imitations in the 1830s and 1840s.

At Stretton and at Nantwich he took the canal across a main road in a short iron trough slung between brick abutments and beautifully curved wing walls (**51**). There are moulded stone piers and dressings. Across the skyline run latticed iron parapet railings. Variants of

this influential design occur on the north Oxford and in starker form on the Tame Valley Canal.

A different and dramatic departure from the norm was the Stanley Ferry Aqueduct on the Aire & Calder (**52**). This is a one-off, designed by the brilliant George Leather and built in 1836–9. The trough and its narrow towpaths hang suspended between two large iron arches. The outsides of the trough are decorated with Greek Revival fluted pilasters, all in cast iron. At either end of the aqueduct there are supporting stone piers hidden behind Doric temple fronts — a strange, inspired touch.

Late-phase aqueducts are utilitarian structures. There are mid-nineteenth-century iron and stone examples on the Cromford, Grand Union and BCN. That on the Cromford is by Stephenson and dates from 1849 and is immediately east of Jessop's ill-starred Wigwell Aqueduct: comparing the two illustrates the changes in design, materials and confidence that took place over 50 years. Three Bridges at Southall on the Grand Union has the canal sandwiched in a trough, between road (above) and railway (below). Frimley Aqueduct on the Basingstoke Canal is an example of sheer functional plainness. It dates from 1839 and takes the canal across a railway line.

In 1893 the old Barton Aqueduct was replaced by a new one. The differences between pioneering Georgian and late Victorian technology could not be greater: Barton old and new are worlds apart. The new aqueduct is a huge, hydraulically driven, iron swing-aqueduct: it opens across the Manchester Ship Canal with water still in its trough (**53**).

Tunnels

Contemporaries found canal tunnels amazing. The experience of travelling underground was regarded with a mixture of fear and delight. It could take hours for a candle-lit boat to pass through a long tunnel. Strange effects were noted by early nineteenth-century tourists. Watching a boat vanish into the maw of Dudley Tunnel, the Reverend Luke Booker reported that its steersman was 'the exact counterpart of Charon'. A visitor to the dark canal-mines of Worsley Delph found bewildering passages and frighteningly low headroom, which made him dizzy. Looking back he saw the distant entrance gleaming 'like a bright star'.

The first British tunnel built for transport purposes was Harecastle on the Trent & Mer-

*53 The new Barton Aqueduct swings open across the Manchester Ship Canal: 1890s canal engineering on the scale of the railways (*RCHME Crown Copyright*).*

sey. It was engineered by Brindley and Henshall and took nine years to complete from 1766 to 1775. It is 2880 yards (2663m) long. By the 1820s this tunnel had become a serious bottleneck and a second 3000-yard long tunnel was built by Telford, in three years, 1824–27. A view of Harecastle Old and Harecastle New Tunnel, side by side, neatly summarizes the differences between Pioneering and Heroic engineering.

Harecastle Old was constructed like an eighteenth-century coal mine. It was bored narrow, cramped and a little wonky, and it had no towpath. Its portal is a simple semicircular hole let into a curving brick wall. Harecastle New was built with a larger bore and a towpath. Its portals were each given a tall arch, with voussoirs, pilasters and a parapet. The contractors for Harecastle New were Pritchard and Hoof, an experienced firm who had already constructed tunnels on the Grand Union, the Regent's and the Lancaster canals. Their brick lining at Harecastle was superb. Telford characteristically descibed the tunnel as 'the most perfect work of its kind yet executed'. In the 50 years that separate Harecastle Old and New many other canal tunnels were built and many lessons learnt about this most arduous aspect of engineering.

Tunnel building involved digging, shoring up, mucking out and lining with bricks. It was dangerous work. Water, fire, collapsing roofs and walls, mud, sand and hard rock were expected hazards. The basic operation was the same for each tunnel. A survey was made and a line pegged out. Drainage headings were dug alongside the line of the tunnel to take away water. Pits were sunk along the intended line at regular intervals. Then miners were sent down and digging began in both directions at the same time. The 'English Method' of tunnelling meant driving a narrow heading or pilot tunnel first which was then extended sideways and downwards to form the tunnel proper.

Construction proceeded with a dogged discipline. As the miners excavated, timber shuttering was put up and spoil was hauled to the surface. Bricklayers followed close behind the miners, lining the tunnel step by step. Water was pumped out as necessary. The well-like working pits were brick-lined and circular, or timber-lined and square. They were usually blocked up after completion of the work. The ventilation shafts standing in the fields above tunnels like Blisworth or Braunston were built much later, after the introduction of powered craft.

Tunnelling was specialized work, not to be undertaken lightly. It was always costly and, as site surveying was not an exact science, often soul-destroying, as the example of Blisworth Tunnel shows. Blisworth was engineered by Jessop, with James Barnes ('a strong-minded man but very illiterate', says the contemporary Hassell) as his assistant. They made surveys and started a tunnel in 1793. In 1796 it was abandoned because of severe flooding. In 1801 a new line was surveyed and Jessop announced that he 'had never come across ground more suitable for tunnelling'. He specified a tunnel 16ft 6in (5m) wide with a brick invert 7ft (2m) below water level and an overall height of

*54 Preston Brook Tunnel, Trent & Mersey Canal: plain Pioneering work of the 1770s (*Alastair Marshall*).*

18ft (5.5m). Work began again and almost immediately encountered problems. The tunnel flooded. The roof collapsed. The contractors proved unsatisfactory. Jessop suggested abandoning the tunnel and building locks instead. But Barnes plodded on and the tunnel was eventually completed in 1805 to Jessop's specifications at a final cost of £70,000. 'Difficult and expensive', noted Telford when he inspected the work. He recommended planting trees to prevent slippage in the tunnel's deep approach cuttings. Apart from the trees there is nothing ornamental at Blisworth — the southern portal of the tunnel (the northern had to be rebuilt in 1903) is ultra-simple: a round arched hole in a brick wall, with 3056 yards (2794m) of darkness beyond it.

Few canal tunnels owned any architectural pretensions. Pioneering examples, which tend to be narrow and fairly short, have simple brick or stone portals and plain wing walls, often rebuilt at a later date. Barnton, Saltersford and Preston Brook (**54**), 1770s tunnels on the Trent & Mersey, are typical. Heroic and Late tunnels, although built to larger dimensions, are usually little different in appearance. A notable exception is Sapperton Tunnel on the Thames & Severn (**55**), completed in 1789 by Josiah Clowes. Both its portals are of Cotswold stone, one a classical triumphal arch, the other crenellated Gothic. Nothing as fanciful as Sapperton's two haunted faces appears again, but in the 1790s a whole cluster of boldly conceived tunnels were built. Some are enlivened with telling details. Greywell on the Basingstoke has brick portals with blind bullseyes. On the Grand Union, Jessop's Braunston (built with an unfortunate kink deep inside) has chunky stone voussoirs at one end. Brandwood on the north Stratford-on-Avon has a brick portal with a symmetrical design consisting of a central stone escutcheon flanked by blind niches, pilasters and blind windows. Its other portal has a stone medallion-bust of Shakespeare. Islington Tunnel, opened in 1820, has imposing brick arched entrances with attenuated voussoirs

55a&b *The two faces of Sapperton Tunnel, Thames & Severn Canal: classical display at one end, Gothic secrecy at the other (*R. Butler; BW Archives*).*

creating a curious expressionist look.

Stone was better than brick for decorative effects. Robert Whitworth's Gannow Tunnel on the Leeds & Liverpool has rusticated portals with outlandish squiggles hammered out of the stonework. His Foulridge Tunnel is a similar design with more conventional rustication around the entrance. Snarestone on the Ashby Canal, open by 1804, has a low profile and rock-faced rustication. Two short stone tunnels — hardly more than extended bridges — stand on the Kennet & Avon in Bath. On each, the portal which faces into the Sydney Gardens stretch is given ornate classical treatment. The setting is intimate, the effect theatrical.

Tunnel building had improved dramatically by the end of the Canal Age. The final years of canal building produced the biggest, most efficient, least-congested tunnels. They were higher and wider than before and had towpaths running through them. This was not an entirely new idea — very short earlier tunnels such as Dunsley, Cookley, and Curdworth also have them. But towpaths could only be built inside longer tunnels once Pioneering construction problems were overcome. Tunnels of the 1830s, like Newbold on the Oxford and Coseley on the BCN New Main Line, had double towpaths for uninterrupted two-way traffic. The last canal tunnel, Netherton, was built in 1855–7 to improve links between the Dudley and the BCN. This mighty passage was driven through shaky, mine-infested ground for 3027 yards (2768m) and was built 27ft (8m) wide at water level. It was lined with blue-grey engineering bricks, has double towpaths and was lit by gas from the beginning.

Horse-paths and legging

Taking a horse-powered boat through a tunnel, especially a long one with no towpath, was unwelcome work. Some of the early tunnels, such as Norwood on the Chesterfield, look unbelievably small from the outside. Inside there was often just room for one boat. It was damp and claustrophobic. And tunnels bred strange stories, fed by the dark journeys and eerie effects. There was always the scary possibility of a boat foundering and sinking deep underground. They were not places for the faint-hearted.

At the entrance to a tunnel with no towpath a horse was unhitched and led away over the top to rejoin its boat on the other side. Several horse-paths survive as rough, dusty tracks running between fields and hedges. Blisworth and Braunston have horse-paths marked by brick ventilation shafts. On the north side of Shrewley Tunnel a separate passage takes the horse-path away at a high level, past houses and across a village street, before descending again to the canal. Husband's Bosworth Tunnel, which opened in 1811, has a perfect horse-path which wanders lyrically between tree-studded hedges. But the finest example of all is linked to Hincaster Tunnel. Set against a background of Cumbrian hills, this is an intriguing system of stone walls, hedges and a steep path, crossed by mini-accommodation bridges as it doglegs up and down above the grand stone tunnel which it was designed in 1817 to serve.

As the horse plodded over the hill, its boat was shafted by poles, pulled along by chains slung from the walls, or more commonly 'legged' through the tunnel. Legging was a process where two men lay along a plank of wood placed across the boat's deck and walked along the tunnel walls to drive the boat forwards. It was usually done by boat crews but occasionally professional leggers were provided by canal companies. Two gangs operated at Blisworth Tunnel between 1827 and 1871, when steam tugs took over. The gangs waited in huts and joined boats as they approached the tunnel. It took hours to leg through a long tunnel and every hour was numbingly the same as the last.

Bodies twisted and legs cramped in the damp air. The effect of candlelit brickwork flicking slowly past was hypnotic. The journalist John Hollingshead was legged through Blisworth Tunnel in 1858. Listening to the boatmen's mournful folk-song and watching the leggers toil away, he found his mind fixed on 'large masses of misery and the utter nothingness of the things of the upper world' (**56**).

56 *Inside Blisworth Tunnel, Grand Union Canal* *(BW Archives)*.

1 *The Kennet & Avon Canal fits into the Bath townscape without a murmur. The iron bridge was cast at Coalbrookdale. The building closing the vista was the canal company headquarters* (R. Butler).

2 *A walled cutting on the Bridgwater & Taunton Canal where it approaches Bridgwater Dock* (R. Butler).

3 (Left) Foxton Locks on the Leicester Line of the Grand Union Canal. Two five-rise staircases scramble up a 75ft-high hill. Built 1810–12 by Benjamin Bevan (R. Butler).

4 (Below) Hillmorton Yard. A view into the Oxford Canal Company's off-line maintenance centre. On the right is the former smithy and the general workshop, now converted into a British Waterways office (R. Butler).

5 (Top right) Plan and elevation of one half of a twin-leaved swing-bridge designed for the Caledonian Canal by Thomas Rhodes; a fine example of a detailed, clean-looking early nineteenth-century drawing. Rhodes was resident engineer on the Caledonian between c.1804 and 1822 (BW Archives).

6 (Bottom right) A prefabricated, cast-iron footbridge, made at Horseley Iron Works, crosses Isis Lock on the Oxford Canal (R. Butler).

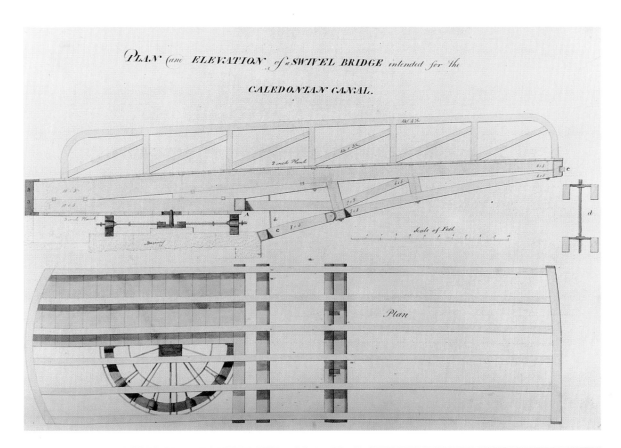

PLAN (and ELEVATION of a SWIVEL BRIDGE intended for the CALEDONIAN CANAL.

Plan

7 *(Left) The aqueduct as triumphal arch; John Rennie's Dundas Aqueduct creates a great sense of occasion and celebrates the Kennet & Avon Canal as it nears the classical city of Bath (R. Butler).*

8 *(Top) Stourport in c.1809. A reconstruction based on contemporary maps and prints (P.Dunn)*

9 *(Bottom) An early nineteenth-century colourwashed drawing of a warehouse (originally two) which still exists on the Calder & Hebble Navigation in Wakefield. A strong, symmetrical design gives prominence to the functional features of loading doors and central boat-hole (BW Archives).*

10 *(Left) Close-up of an Aire & Calder warehouse in the redeveloped dock quarter of Leeds. Crisp details of sack-hoist pulley, loading doors, platforms and regularly-spaced windows* (R. Butler).

11 *(Right) A canal house at Saul Junction, a bridge-keeping, toll-collecting point where the Gloucester & Sharpness crosses the Stroudwater Canal. The attached office, the picket fence, and the overall plainness are typical* (R. Butler).

12 *A cottage, a pub, and a warehouse form a knot of interest at Fradley Junction, where the Coventry Canals joins the Trent & Mersey. Canal junctions were often places where small communities grew and buildings for living and working rubbed shoulders* (R. Butler).

13 (*Above*) *Tooley's Yard at Banbury on the Oxford Canal. The ramshackle, make-do-and-mend world of a small boatyard. The dry dock and smithy date from the eighteenth century, the carpenter's shop is later* (R. Butler).

14 (*Left*) *A blend of colour, fantasy and homely detail in a world of brick and smoke; narrow boats are as typical of England's canals as gondolas are of Venice* (R. Butler).

4

Docks, ports and wharfs

Situated along England's waterways were nodal points where boats came and went. There were river ports and sea ports; there were canal ports which fitted into old towns or mushroomed into new ones, and there were hundreds of docks, basins and wharfs in industrial cities, market towns and villages. The size and scale of these places varied but their purpose was essentially the same. From Duke's Dock to Tavistock, Gas Street to Honey Street, Cuckoo Wharf to Etruria, waterborne goods were loaded, unloaded, stored or trans-shipped onto other boats or other forms of transport.

By the 1720s Defoe estimated that there were 1160 miles (1867km) of navigable waterway in Great Britain. Descriptions in his lively *Tour* are scattered with key words: 'trade, business, merchants, coal and corn, ships, barges, ports, wharfs, warehouses'. The last two in particular had come by the early eighteenth century to signify a recognizable pattern of development which can still be seen today. That pattern was linear: where a river wound through a town's port area, its banks were reinforced with stone and timber, forming wharfs. Upon these wharfs, either flush with the bank or set back behind a quay, were warehouses, cranes and sheds. Behind these were streets containing living accommodation packed around with pubs, shops, stores, stables, barns, smithies, sail lofts and carpenters, shops, providing all the burly accessories of a port.

The most impressive buildings Defoe would have seen in a river port were multi-storey warehouses. Places like Boston, Newark, Gainsborough and Wisbech had riversides crowded with batteries of grain and seed warehouses. There was no uniform size or shape, just the best use made of the available space. Typically these warehouses had load-bearing walls of brick, with pantile roofs. Inside there were wooden floors supported on wooden posts, providing uninterrupted floor space. Elevations were simple — rows of windows interrupted by loading doors set one above another. Designed purely for use, the architecture of these buildings was frontal and wholesome. They were the precursors of warehouse types that developed to serve canals.

Canal warehouses can be roughly divided into three main types: the common lay-by warehouse where a boat tied alongside, often beneath a canopy; the boat-hole warehouse, where a boat entered through an arched opening, and the straddle warehouse, a rare and often beautiful type which spanned a waterway, allowing boats to pass freely beneath. Examples of all these functional warehouse types survive, standing at the canal side, clustered at navigation heads or wharfs, and grouped in ranks at once-busy docks.

Canal docks at seaports

Docks developed from the eighteenth century as a way of organizing the storage and trans-shipment of goods from sea-going ships to

57 *Regent's Canal Dock (Limehouse Basin) in the 1960s: a trans-shipment dock cluttered with low ranges of sheds and the sharp shapes of cranes, barges and sea-going ships. At the top is the Thames, at bottom right the Regent's Canal (*BW Archives*).*

inland lighters and barges. Large ports like London and Liverpool were served by a network of rivers and canals, which in a few cases required their own docks as part of the larger port system. In London the Regent's Canal Company built a dock at Limehouse in the 1820s (**57**). It still remains the terminus for the canal. Elmes's *Metropolitan Improvements* (1827) shows contemporary views of Regent's Canal Dock — ships at anchor and barges being poled across the water; piles of Baltic timber, indistinct buildings and a capstan-operated swing bridge across the entrance. General merchandise and raw materials were trans-shipped here, on their way to Midlands and Northern factories. On the other side of the Thames the Grand Surrey Canal, which received its Act in 1801, formed part of a busy trans-shipment system which in 1864 became Surrey Commercial Docks. Between 1799 and 1805, the short-cut known as the Isle of Dogs Canal was turned into a vast linear quay flanked by the majestic buildings of West India Docks, London's pride, the largest docks on earth.

Like London, the port of Liverpool grew rapidly in the eighteenth century. Between the 1690s and the 1790s, considerable waterway development opened Liverpool to hinterland trade and markets. Its docks became a key outlet for trade on the Mersey, Weaver, Mersey and Irwell Navigation, Douglas Navigation, St Helen's Canal, Bridgewater Canal and Leeds & Liverpool Canal. This growth in inland waterway traffic was reflected by the building of Manchester Dock and Chester Dock by Liverpool Corporation in the late eighteenth century. By 1825 Manchester Dock was shifting about 1,000 tons of goods daily – mainly trans-shipped from coasters into barges. In 1773 the Bridgewater Co. began Duke's Dock as the Liverpool terminus (via the Mersey) for Bridgewater and Trent and Mersey canal cargoes.

Duke's was a trans-shipment dock, dealing mainly in grain and cotton. It was rectangular in shape and fairly small. Its designer may have been John Gilbert, the Duke's versatile agent, whilst Thomas Wallwork was responsible for the chunky sandstone walls. The earliest warehouse built there was an eight-storey block put up in 1780–83. But more significant, architecturally, was Grain Warehouse of 1811 (**58**). This was a remarkable brick and stone building, with a symmetrical elevation divided into ten bays. The central two bays were pedimented and spanned a pair of semicircular boat holes set within a larger semi-circle which was rusticated and punctuated with bull's-eye windows: a powerful Palladian design. The boat holes, for internal loading, displayed a family resemblance to earlier Bridgewater Company warehouses built in Manchester. These arched entrances were both functional and logical, given the relative size of waterway craft. They are a feature that occurs again and again on canals throughout England. Grain Warehouse was significant for another reason: it was iron-framed. Cast-iron beams, arches and columns all went into its construction.

Iron and brick played an even more potent

58 *The warehouse as architecture: big pediment and sturdily detailed boat holes. Grain Warehouse looms over the cramped, water-filled spaces of Duke's Dock, Liverpool. Built 1811, now demolished (*RCHME Crown Copyright*).*

part in the warehouses designed for the Leeds & Liverpool's 1840s' terminus at Stanley Dock. These cyclopean blocks were the work of Jesse Hartley, an engineer who designed with real guts and intelligence. Stanley Dock warehouses are grittier versions of Hartley's famous Albert Dock. The architecture is simple and sublime, as befits a great seaport. But it has more to do with nautical than canal traditions.

More typical of canals were the docks built in association with sea-links and ship canals: Grangemouth and Bowling on the Forth & Clyde; the remote and beautiful little basin at Crinan; Port Carlisle on the ill-fated Carlisle Canal, and the docks at Glasson, Heybridge, Ulverston and Bridgwater. Most of these were unspectacular: a sea-lock and a canal lock, with a stone-lined basin in between, a warehouse or two, sheds or open coal floors, a few cottages, sometimes a lighthouse.

Glasson Dock began in the 1780s as an extension to the small river port of Lancaster. Between 1819 and 1825 a Glasson Dock branch was added to the Lancaster Canal, and a large

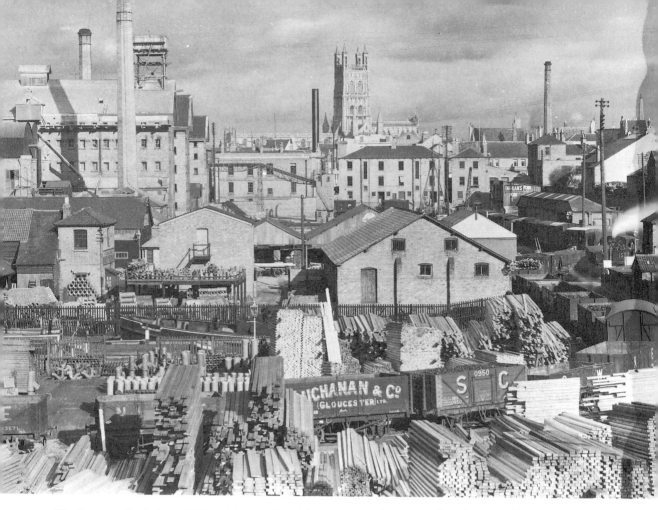

59 *Gloucester Docks in c. 1925: multi-textured, multi-layered; buildings, boats, cargoes, goods trains — one kind of activity superimposed upon another (*RCHME Crown Copyright*).*

new canal basin was added to the original one. In its wake came housing, a school and a chapel. Bridgwater Dock provides a more interesting example of a hand-worked dock linking the Bridgwater & Taunton Canal with the River Parrett. The dock was opened on a sunny day in March 1841 at a ceremony enlivened by cannon, streamers, and 'a vast number of the fair sex'. The dock is not large. The canal locks into an inner basin. Beyond this is a tidal basin, ringed by an amazing number of black paddle stands — part of a later system of scouring sluices. There were two locks from the river; one for ships, the other for barges. A terrace of dock-workers' houses, a large rectangular brick

warehouse and a later mill building survive, but the industries the dock served — the coal, pottery, and timber yards clustered along the river Parrett — have gone. In the 1980s, the dock was redeveloped as a marina surrounded by housing.

Redevelopment has altered the character of the Gloucester & Sharpness, but this windswept waterway starts and finishes in two large dock complexes, one of which, Sharpness, is still in commercial use. Sharpness Old Dock was built in the 1820s: a small stone-walled basin with a house, stables and sea wall. It is simply detailed and sheltered by the wooded bluff of Lord Berkeley's Pleasure Grounds. In the 1870s Old Dock was extended when the large New Dock was built. New Dock has a curving basin lined with brick warehouses, old railway sidings and timber wharfs. Its original warehouses (one survives) were very impressive. Almost the last word in multistorey warehouse design, they were similar to those put up at Gloucester Docks (**59**) during the great building campaigns of the 1830s to 1890s.

Gloucester had been a port since Roman times, but only with the opening of the ship canal could ocean-going vessels (600 tonners) reach the city and trans-ship into the barges and trows which plied the higher reaches of the Severn. Docks were begun and the main basin was built by 1812. After a slow start due to delays over opening the canal, the corn warehouses were built. As a group, these are spectacular (**60**). North Warehouse was built in 1826, Biddles, Shiptons, Lock and Pillar warehouses in the 1830s, Herbert, Kimberley, Phillpotts, Vinings and Sturges in the accelerated building campaign which followed repeal of the Corn Laws in the 1840s. In 1873 Llanthony, the last and biggest, was built. All these warehouses were of similar appearance and construction: tall, multi-storey boxes with load-bearing brick walls and wide, uninterrupted timber floors, with wooden beams and joists, supported on wooden or cast iron posts. They have pitched slate roofs, tiers of boarded loading doors and regularly spaced, barred or shuttered windows. Hand-worked sack hoists were fitted into rooftop lucams or jigger rooms (**61**). Typically one of these warehouses could hold about 20,000 sacks of grain, carefully stacked so as not to overload the floors.

A contract for North Warehouse (built by William Rees and Son) stipulated use of local bricks in Flemish bond, Bath or Forest stone sills, large blue Welsh slates and Memel or Danzig timber. Despite the use of similar materials, the Gloucester warehouses are not identical. Pillar Warehouse is the most dignified: a twin-gabled symmetrical elevation with a colonnade of iron columns flush with the quayside for direct ship-to-shore goods handling. Llanthony is the most diagrammatic, with a total height of eight storeys and a sharp rhythm of oblong windows counterpointing the vertical lines of loading doors. These buildings

60 *Warehouses at Gloucester Docks: architectural beauty derived from mass, silhouette and light-and-shade effects of void and solid* (RCHME Crown Copyright).

are uncompromisingly direct. Their contact with boats and water is immediate. The clarity and geometry of their silhouettes and the drama created by their different orientations is unforgettable.

By the mid-nineteenth century Gloucester was one of England's major corn ports. Con

61 *Attic storey of Llanthony Warehouse, Gloucester Docks: roof slates on battins, queen-post trusses, hand-worked gear for winding up sacks* (RCHME Crown Copyright).

temporary maps show the effect which the flourishing docks had on the city. Along the canal and river approaches there are spin-off industries: boat-builders' yards, timber yards, coal yards, rope-walks, mills, foundries, a gas works and pubs with simple sailors' names — the Mermaid, the Ship, the Star, the Globe. On the western edge of the city, with gardens on one side and river meadows on the other, are the docks, with the still-growing ancillary features: the barge arm, Victoria Dock, graving docks, railways, open sheds, offices and work-shops all fitted around the dark-shaded ware-houses and the Mariners' Chapel — a poignant reminder that this was a port where seafaring and waterway traditions met and overlapped and went their separate ways again.

Inland ports

Runcorn, Ellesmere Port, Goole and Stourport are examples of inland canal ports where small towns developed on empty or green-field sites. Leland described Runcorn in the sixteenth century as 'a poor townlet by a salt creke'. In the 1770s the Duke of Bridgewater extended his canal to a point just beyond this 'townlet' and established a port there. A flight of ten broad locks stepped down to the Mersey. A small tidal dock was built at the bottom, and a basin at the top of the flight. A warehouse and two rows of workers' cottages were built. Finally the Duke erected a large house for himself, overlooking his small port.

Runcorn formed an important link with the Potteries. It imported clay, flint and bonemeal, and exported pots, along with stone and potatoes, to Liverpool and Manchester. But it had one problem, which was shallow water. By the end of the eighteenth century a new basin and river lock had been built. In the nineteenth century further extensions took place at Run-corn and rival companies — the Mersey & Irwell Navigation and the Weaver Navi-gation — built their own docks nearby. The Weaver Navigation's Weston Point Docks included warehouses, stables, housing and a

hotel. By 1841 this paternalistic company had added a church with a parsonage and a school. Parson, schoolmaster and church choir were all on the company payroll. At the same time the Duke's original Runcorn expanded. A visiting engineer noted 'lofty warehouses, extensive wharfs, docks, and basins'. For a brief period Runcorn was fashionable as a resort and was dubbed the 'Montpellier of England'. But by 1850 burgeoning salt and chemical industries and a lack of planning had driven the tourists away.

Ellesmere Port, at the Mersey end of the Shropshire Union Canal, began as a modestly scaled trans-shipment centre in c. 1802. Between 1828 and 1843, the port was redeveloped to designs made by Telford and largely carried out by William Cubitt. Two basins on different levels and an inner dock connected river and canal. Onto this site were built warehouses, offices, stables, workshops, engine houses, a lighthouse and dockers' cottages. The out-standing building here was the E-plan Winged Warehouse, which straddled part of the inner dock, allowing undercover loading. It was an imaginative solution to a practical problem —

62 *Winged Warehouse, Ellesmere Port: built in the 1820s, gutted by fire and demolished in the 1970s. A convincing, articulate design; barges pulled underneath and were loaded directly from the storage floors above (BW; Arthur Watts Collection).*

that of a cramped split-level site — and a fine example of Telford's severe style. In 1843 Ellesmere Port was advertised as having 'one hundred houses, an extensive range of first class Warehouses, a Noble Dock with Wharfs, Shipbuilders' Yards etc'. The pattern of activity was the same here as elsewhere — transshipping took place between canal boats and coasters and sailing ships. As at Runcorn, industry followed the establishment of the canal port, which in turn grew prosperous and was enlarged in the mid- to late nineteenth century. A small amount of company housing was built from the 1830s in the dock area. In the 1870s, 1880s and 1890s the canal company expanded the housing stock, acted as a school governor and assisted in the provision of churches, a mission hut and a new gasworks.

Ellesmere Port is a serious-looking place, built of Cheshire bricks, Welsh slate and iron. There is still plenty of hard-edged texture and surfacing to be seen. The self-contained character of the place is heightened by the enclosing buildings and changing levels of the site. At the heart of the port is the Toll Office. To either side are stables, workshops and a pattern shop. The Pump House with its wooden accumulator tower supplied hydraulic power to the port, which was lit by gas in the 1860s for night-time working. Telford's great Winged Warehouse (**62**) was gutted by fire in the 1970s and had to be demolished. But the single storey China Clay Shed of 1846, and the Island Warehouse of 1871, survive as part of the Boat Museum.

Goole was a planned port. Built where the new Knottingley and Goole Canal joined the Ouse, it threatened Hull's regional dominance, and caused the old port of Selby to decline. From Goole, Yorkshire goods were exported to places as far away as Archangel and America. The new port was constructed in the 1820s and '30s by the Aire & Calder Navigation Co. Its designer was the versatile George Leather. The contractors were Jolliffe & Banks, the first pre-railway large-scale civil engineering firm.

63 *Goole in coal-carrying days: dusty 'Tom puddings', lofty coal hoists and a raw, ambiguous horizon of mills, warehouses and company town (*BW; Arthur Watts Collection*).*

Before building began, 200 acres (81ha) of land were purchased and a hamlet was swept away. The port was tightly designed: a square dock area with a wedge-shaped new town above. On its east side ran the River Ouse, on its west lay fields and sparsely inhabited fens. The site was bleak, the architecture raw. The working port area was built with a basin, a ship dock and a barge dock. Warehouses and sheds were built, followed by offices, a custom house, a boat repair yard and housing for agents and dock staff.

Although the Aire & Calder Co. leased land for building they kept a firm control on development. Leather's original guidelines produced uniform streets of brick and slate houses and the new town was zoned. Aire Street and Ouse Street contained shops, pubs, offices, and a market. East Parade was posh. Poorer terraces began near the centre and were pushed away northwards. At the social hub of the town were the Public Rooms, Commercial Buildings and the Lowther Hotel. A church was not built until the 1840s. The company provided schools, a Literary and Scientific Society and a fair, as well as laying on essential services including sewers, waterworks, gasworks and a fire brigade.

When the railways came, Goole grew. The port area was enlarged and heavy equipment, like the outlandish coal hoists, was introduced (**63**). Later, new terraces and wider streets were built. Goole remains a remote-seeming town, but its docks still work, affording the visitor glimpses of that most poignant of contrasts, big ships and small houses.

The greatest of all canal-inspired towns is Stourport — 'a complete Maritime town in the very heart of the Kingdom... a new creation', an historic mix of water, boats and buildings (**64**, see **8**). Stourport was the Staffs & Worcester's trans-shipment port, its River Severn terminus, which almost put Bewdley out of business as soon as it opened. In 1769, the canal company bought two riverside fields and river locks and a basin had been laid out, probably to the elder Dadford's designs, by 1771. After that, Stourport's growth was dramatic. In the 1780s the two lower basins and Clock Basin

were constructed. In the early nineteenth century a further basin (now filled in) was added. The famous print of 1776 shows an early view with the Tontine Hotel and its riverside gardens given pride of place. The Tontine was Stourport's unofficial business centre. In and around it, in a typically Georgian way, revolved the life and work of the port. Warehousing, storage and dock facilities, and a small number of houses were built. Other buildings appeared as need arose. Long Warehouse and Iron Warehouse were amongst the earliest. Clock Warehouse, a rectangular brick and slate building, was also late eighteenth-century. Its wooden clock-tower was added in 1812. Stables, a boat repair yard with a dry dock, and the Engine Basin (for use from the river only) were added later. As usual, industry followed the canal, dotting it with warehouses, sheds and landings as it headed up and away from the river towards the Black Country.

Stourport was not a planned town. The canal company built some three-storey brick houses in Mart Lane, probably for its staff, and it may have gone in for some property development of its own, but most of Stourport is spec-built, its unity of style owing much to Georgian traditions and the use of pattern-books. The area wedged between the canal and Bridge Street contains the best buildings. Brick mansions with big, vaulted cellars and access to the wharfs were built in York Street, overlooking the basins — Georgian merchants liked to live close to their work and wealth. In the late eighteenth century, the 'smart set' came to Stourport and stayed until industry and boredom drove them away. The orderly, understated houses they used have been knocked about and modern accretions lend Stourport a faded air. But there is still a lot going on. There are close-walled winding lanes, enclosed backyards, tousled corners, sudden edges, and glimpses of water between jumbled sheds. Coloured boats and slim river cruisers act as mobile foils to the static time-worn textures of brick, timber and iron. The pleasing decay, the

64 *Georgian Stourport: Clock Warehouse and Middle Basin overlooked by smart housing (*BW; Arthur Watts Collection*).*

ambiguous, insular character of canal places like this needs to be savoured while it still can be.

Shardlow is a miniature version of Stourport. Nicknamed 'Little Liverpool', it developed as a trans-shipment point between the River Trent and the Trent & Mersey Canal from the 1770s onwards. Numerous warehouses were built (**65**) along with a boatyard and industrial premises for malting, brewing, corn-milling and rope making. There were pubs, rows of workers' cottages and handsome houses for Shardlow's boat-owning merchants — the Suttons, Soresbys, and Flacks. Malt, corn, cheese, salt, iron, lead and coal were stored in or exported from the red brick warehouses whose reconditioned

65 *Warehouse at Shardlow: classical pediment above functional boat hole; the stripped but lingering 'politeness' of late eighteenth-century industrial buildings* (R. Butler)

or decaying carcasses lie scattered at various angles to the canal. These warehouses are small (by later standards) and their appearance reflects the best Midlands traditions of early industrial vernacular; several have semi-circular windows with iron-framed fanlights, a domestic motif which in this context is nonsensical but charming. The warehouses were served by lay-bys or basins. Two of them at least had boat holes for internal loading. One of these is Trent Corn Mill No. 2, dated 1780, a symmetrical Palladian block with pedimented centre and a broad, segmental-arched boat-hole.

Canal towns such as Shardlow grew organically around their waterfronts. There were numerous contemporary references to the tendency. By 1773 Worsley, starting-point of the Bridgewater Canal, was reported to have 'the appearance of a considerable Sea port town ...'. And in the 1780s the 'wharfs and busy traffic' gave Stone, on the Trent & Mersey, 'the lively aspect of a little seaport'. As time goes on, the imagery becomes less attractive. Sir George Head, touring the manufacturing districts of england in the 1830s, found himself on a packet boat near Runcorn enjoying the 'panorama of cows, cottages and green fields'. But leaning out of the boat he noticed that the canal was as 'black as the Styx' and 'smelt villainous'.

Industrial wharfs and warehouses

Telford wrote in 1804 that the main purpose of canals was for 'Conveying Fuel and Raw Materials to ... Manufacturing Towns and Districts, and Exporting the Manufactured Goods'. Canalside sites were vital to the success of all kinds of industries — textile mills, potteries, collieries, maltings, ironworks and so on. The image of a canal slinking through the sooty maze of an industrial city is an archetypal one. Visiting Manchester in the early nineteenth century, the German architect Schinkel was astounded at what he found. In his diary he made drawings of towering mill blocks, with canal and river boats in the foreground. Contemporary prints and early photographs

66 *Hall & Rogers' 1836 warehouse at junction of Rochdale and Ashton Canals: the sublime, Manchester effect of bleak brick walling pierced by running lines of small, round-arched windows (*RCHME Crown Copyright*).*

show the same thing. There are images of chaotic urban blight, of billowing smoke, boat-haunted wharfs and brackish factory basins. There are clustered chimneys above gaunt fields and blasted heaths, black sheds and weary terraces of housing; awesome scenes which for a time existed nowhere else on earth. In Lancashire and Yorkshire, textile mills were built right at the water's edge, with loading doors that opened directly onto a boat's deck. Staffordshire potworks relied heavily on canals for transporting their raw materials and finished goods. Wedgwood had fought like mad in the 1760s to get the Trent & Mersey to pass his Etruria factory. Brindley's brother established a potworks at Longport in the 1770s. Shirley's Etruscan Bone and Flint Mill got its own canal arm in the 1850s: its irregular, squashed site included single-storey sheds, a crane and narrow brick-paved landings alongside the canal. Middleport Pottery was built in 1888 on an empty Trent & Mersey site. Its arrival was followed by a wharf, a boatyard

and terraced housing in a classic and very late example of the pattern of a canal attracting industry which in turn acted as a catalyst for further growth.

Apart from such self-serving examples, big industrial towns also had many public, private and company-owned wharfs and basins. By the 1920s, the $8\frac{1}{2}$ miles (14km) long Regent's Canal had over 200 wharfs leased or belonging to companies as diverse as Bass & Co., Finsbury Borough Council, Fellows Morton & Clayton Ltd., Gas Light & Coke Co., Thorley's Food for Cattle, Westinghouse, Woolworth, several railway companies, etc. Early nineteenth-century maps of Birmingham show orchards and 'Small Gardens' bordering much of the course of the Birmingham and the Worcester & Birmingham canals. By 1840, on a two-mile (3km) stretch of the Birmingham & Fazeley there were 124 wharfs and canalside industries. Ackermann's 'Panoramic View' of 1847 shows buildings and chimneys sprouting along the encircling canals. In the late nineteenth-century, the last congested half-mile of the BCN Main Line contained 2 general wharfs, 12 basins and numerous industrial premises: a mixture of railway, mill, chemical, iron foundry, general carrying and public wharfs. One canalside warehouse — Shipton's — remains. A long rectangular building with central loading doors and cambered arch windows, it was built in 1842 bang on the canalside. Of Birmingham's three biggest wharfs, Old Wharf and Worcester Wharf have gone and Gas Street Basin, once an enclosed, secretive canal zone, has been blown open by modern development. Of the great railway/canal trans-shipment sheds and factory docks (such as the Borax Soapworks where boats nosed their way deep inside) little now remains.

In Manchester a group of warehouses survives in the Castlefield area, where the rivers Medlock and Irwell and the Bridgewater and Rochdale canals link together. This is the earliest terminus of the Bridgewater Canal and here in the 1760s and 1770s early multi-storey

67 *A roofed-in wharf, with gas lights and hydraulic cranes: inside the Great Northern Railway Co's. transshipment warehouse on the Regent's Canal. From the* Illustrated London News *(BW Archives).*

warehouses were built. Grocer's Warehouse, for example, had round-arched windows and boat-holes which influenced the design of later Castlefield warehouses like Merchant's Warehouse and Middle Warehouse, where the great two-into-one arch feature recalls the striking Grain Warehouse of Duke's Dock, Liverpool. Hall & Rogers' Rochdale Canal warehouse in Tarriff Street belongs to the same Manchester family. Dated 1836, it is a stripped brick block, with an almost total lack of detail (**66**). The Rochdale Canal Co. had its head office in Dale Street, with a paved wharf area reached through a castellated gateway. The wharf included another warehouse, also with twin boat-holes. The last canal warehouses to be built in Manchester, as elsewhere, were for

railway/canal trans-shipment. The GNR Goods Warehouse in Watson Street, a fine example built in 1898, linked the Manchester & Salford Junction Canal with the railway on two levels inside the building. The GNR specialized in Italianate blockbusters — they built another equally impressive one at Camden Lock on the Regent's Canal (**67**).

There was no discussion — none whatsoever — about canal architecture in 'polite' architectural circles. Yet warehouse designs of real quality were produced. Rennie drew some elegant elevations. Telford saw a number of his built. An early nineteenth-century Calder & Hebble warehouse in Wakefield is especially memorable. Here the boat-hole has become a grand entrance and the loading doors are framed by big relieving arches (see **9**). The great Aire & Calder warehouse which once stood in Call Lane, Leeds, had an unbeatable scale and drama. Another Leeds example is the

68 *Flyboat Warehouse, Aire & Calder Dock, Leeds, c. 1830. A 'palazzo' type warehouse with a dramatically broken up wall space. A strong rhythm of large and small openings is created by loading doors, windows and arches which originally formed an open arcade. The building has now been converted to living accommodation (*RCHME Crown Copyright*).*

Flyboat Warehouse which seems to refer — in its strong rhythm of arches and squares — to Renaissance designs (**68**). And the Terminal Warehouse at Sheffield Basin, which punctuated the canal vista until obscured by the later Straddle Warehouse, has a cave-like entrance beneath a romantically inflated giant pediment. These are examples which display a real feeling for form, texture and silhouette without ever departing from strictly functional requirements. Drama of an accidental kind is found where there is a sudden or unexpected change of scale — at Nottingham, where the late nineteenth century Fellows Morton and Clayton Wharf is overshadowed by a huge slab-block warehouse of the early twentieth century, or at Coventry Basin, where boats enter suddenly into a wide, walled yard after squeezing beneath a narrow, toy-like bridge. Here there are warehouses with doors which fold back and lie flush in purpose-made brick recesses.

At the southern end of the Grand Union, at Nash Mills, Apsley and Brentford, there are giant sheds, steel framed and steel clad, with pitched roofs and huge canopies overhanging the water (**69**). These were built in the 1950s and 1960s, the final austere examples of a functional tradition which stretches back to the awning-fronted warehouses that crowded City Road and Paddington Basins (**70**) as long ago as the early 1800s.

Canal basins where warehouses and sheds are grouped with other buildings survive in former industrial towns and villages. Limestone and lime were exported from Bugsworth Basin on the Peak Forest Canal. Here there was a large complex of wharfs, warehouses, stables, tramroad sidings and lime kilns. Nearby at Whaley Bridge, where the Peak Forest Canal and the Cromford & High Peak Railway joined, a trans-shipment dock was constructed. This single-storey stone building encloses a canal dock flanked by railway tracks; its interior is clearly expressed by the external appearance of three arches beneath three gables. At Sowerby Bridge, where the Rochdale joined the Calder & Hebble, trans-Pennine cargoes were transshipped or stored. Three late-eighteenth-century stone warehouses, one with an internal

69 *Big dumb sheds: twentieth-century warehousing —*
steel-framed, with steel clad canopies — at Croxley Mills
*on the Grand Union Canal (*BW Archives*).*

dock, an agent's house, stables and a mid-
nineteenth-century weigh-house form an interesting group against a backcloth of rainy hills
and vacant industrial sites.

    Away to the south in another industrialized

70 *Paddington Basin in 1801: commercial scene as fete.*
Between weatherboarded, canopied sheds a narrow boat
unloads, a packet boat leaves, men work, tourists loaf: the
*relaxed life of Georgian England (*BW Archives*).*

valley, Brimscombe Port formed a trans-shipment point on the Thames and Severn Canal.
There was a big multi-purpose building here,
a warehouse/office/agent's house combined,
smaller warehouses, a boat-gauge, coal wharf
and forge. Like Sowerby Bridge, Brimscombe
was also stone-built and its buildings reflected
local forms and features — in this case those of
Stroud Valley mills and the Cotswolds. On the
Leeds & Liverpool, Eanam Wharf in Blackburn, built in the early nineteenth century,
presents a tightly-packed site. Its landside is
enclosed by walls and railings, its canalside
fronted by stone and weatherboarded ware-

houses, with canal houses and offices tucked in behind. Again the dominant material is stone — stone setts in the yard, stone flags and kerbs along the canalside, stone slates on the roofs.

Smaller town wharfs

In 1782 John Gott, resident engineer on the Selby Canal, was told to build a 'Counting House, Warehouse, Crane, Rigging House, Tarring House, Sailmaker's Shop and a Place for depositing old Ropes at Selby'. Gott's buildings have not survived, but in out-of-the-way market towns such as Louth and Great Driffield there are navigation heads with the remains of commercial areas and basins. Louth's riverhead has prominently sited warehouses dating from the late eighteenth century. They are built of small red bricks and have steeply pitched roofs with coped gables. Nearby granaries, cottages and a pub recall the days when Louth built ships and boasted more corn merchants than Grimsby. Great Driffield's riverhead has a similar, more coherent group of mills, warehouses and cranes. Town and larger village wharfs often specialized in handling local produce — there are granaries at Newbury and Devizes and cheese warehouses at Nantwich and Ellesmere. Coal for household and industrial use was landed everywhere. At its Shrewsbury terminus in the 1830s, the Shrewsbury Canal Co. built a warehouse-cum-market with a Greek Revival portico and rendered walls hiding a functional iron and timber-framed interior — a common arrangement probably influenced by the design of contemporary corn exchanges.

A town wharf had a life of its own, apart from the community and industries it served. It was a place with its own habits, smells — coal, lime, manure — and sounds: the muffled thump of wooden boats being poled and budged, the jingle of a horse and cart, the sudden rattle of a hand-operated crane. No airs, no graces, no glamour, just occasional, unintended effects of light and shadow — a tarred gable, a whitewashed doorway — and

plenty of crunchy texture. There were floor-scapes of cobbles or setts, rough-tooled copings butting directly onto water, shiny mooring cleats, and bollards worn and scuffed with use. Water articulated the space between buildings; the bustle of work and the moving colours and shapes of boats brought them to life. Middling towns such as Grantham and Market Harborough, Skipton and Kendal had their own flourishing basins and wharfs. At Cuckoo Wharf in Worksop (**71**) a fine, buff brick warehouse, survivor of a type which was once more common, straddles the Chesterfield Canal. Telford's General Warehouse at Ellesmere Port and the steel-framed Straddle Warehouse at Sheffield Basin used the same idea. Newtown, at the Welsh end of the Montgomery Canal, had a rectangular basin which in the mid-nineteenth century was surrounded by wharfs leased to tenants, many of whom were in the lime trade. Here there were workaday buildings of all kinds, from warehouses to pigsties. And scattered along this agricultural canal were over 80 small, private wharfs, many having cottages which still exist.

Village and country wharfs

A barge full of hay, narrow boats bursting with grain, coal or manure, decks piled with cabbages or packed with milk churns: these were typical loads picked up and set down at country wharfs. Canal wharfs became locked into their local and regional economies. There were wharfs alongside farms, mills, brickyards, limeworks and quarries; wharfs which created new settlements of their own, and wharfs in places where a canal carved its way through an existing village which became re-orientated around the new line of life and activity. This happened most spectacularly at Shardlow, but there are other examples like Braunston, Blisworth, and Stoke Bruerne, which were reshaped by the Grand Union Canal.

Blisworth and Stoke Bruerne are two Northamptonshire villages separated by fields and a canal tunnel. In 1796 the *Northampton Mercury*

71 *An elegant solution to the problem of a tight site: a rare straddle warehouse spanning the Chesterfield Canal at Cuckoo Wharf, Worksop (R. Butler).*

reported 'extensive wharfage & warehouses ... two new inns ... five or six thousand tons of coal ... a large number of coal-boats and trading boats' at Blisworth. There was a mill here, rebuilt in its present form in the 1870s. Beside it stands an earlier warehouse on the site of a Pickford's wharf which took advantage of a canal/turnpike road junction. Long-distance and local goods were trans-shipped here and taken by road as far east as Cambridge and by water as far as Birmingham, Bath, Oxford and London. On the other side of the tunnel, the canal cuts a swathe through the middle of Stoke Bruerne, which, after the boats arrived, turned into a flourishing industrial village. It has now become a celebrated set piece, with many of its canalside buildings adapted to new uses and much of its industrial history still traceable on the ground.

Equally intriguing are wharfs on edge-of-village or green-field sites, places where there was either very little or nothing at all before a canal arrived. On the Kennet & Avon at Honey Street, a cluster of battered sheds, scattered houses and a pub exist because Robbins & Co. established a private wharf here in 1811 to build barges and provide a general service to the agricultural industry. Kilby on the Leicester Line was a new settlement with two pubs, a coalyard, a company engineer's house and some cottages. Tardebigge New Wharf on the Worcester & Birmingham was established around 1810. Sited between the top of the great lock flight and the tunnel, New Wharf consisted of a basin serving lime kilns and coal merchants. The surviving stone warehouse was built by John Smith, a local 'stone-getter', and the stone came from a quarry immediately nearby. A plain rectangular building of two storeys, it stands gable end on to the canal and its walls are two feet thick. A weighing machine was installed at the wharf and cottages were built at the back of the roughly triangular site, their plain and painted brick walls forming a foil to the sharp angles of the later maintenance yard and its crane. A larger, early twentieth-century canal house closes the site on its eastern side. New Wharf had a wharfinger and a warehouseman to supervise use of its facilities. Sometimes a wharfinger's cottage was tacked on to a warehouse. Pewsey, a company-owned wharf on the Kennet & Avon, is a good

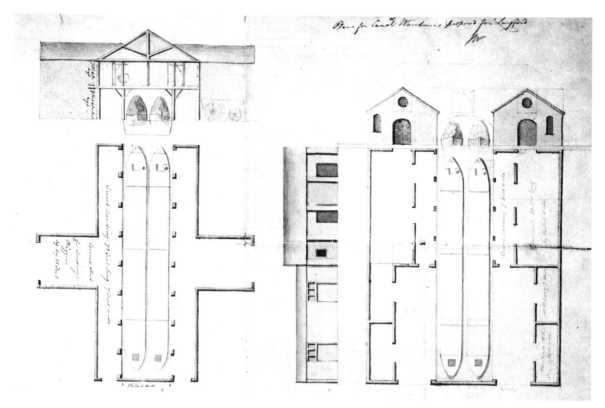

72 *A plan for a warehouse on the Coventry Canal: a symmetrical, agricultural-looking design of c. 1800, with boat hole, covered dock, cranes, and storage space (*BW Archives*).*

example; a long brick building with its storage part towards the water and its cottage furthest away from it; a neat, cheap design with an unbroken roofline.

A wharfinger's job was a busy one. By the mid-nineteenth century, his paperwork was enormous and his duties often included gauging boats as well as maintaining records of loads, deliveries and stored items. Records from Wappenshall Junction, where a brick warehouse stands on the derelict Newport Branch, list fruit, furniture, glass, soap, wine, coffee, building materials, limestone, coal and gunpowder. Harmless goods like cheese or salt might be left in a warehouse for weeks at a time, but gunpowder was generally unpopular with wharfingers and its lengthy storage was not encouraged.

The inside of a rural warehouse was very plain (**72**): bare brick or stone walls, paved or earth ground floor, wooden stairways, boarded upper floor and an open roof, usually with queen-post or king-post trusses, purlins and rafters. Doors were sturdily planked. Windows were small and fitted with shutters or slatted ventilators through which dim light fell across bales and barrows and sacks. Rural warehouses varied considerably. Some aped grand styles. The tiny Westport Canal (opened in 1840, closed 1875) insisted on a Palladian elevation for its terminal warehouse (**73**). Humbler-looking examples now seem incredibly small, like the timber-framed trans-shipment warehouse at Rednal, a tight, hole-in-the-corner wharf on the Montgomery. Even smaller are farm wharf survivors along the Grand Union, Shropshire Union and Oxford: just open yards, occasionally graced by a brick shed with a door opening onto the canal.

Since the Second World War changes in the industrial and commercial life of England have been huge. There is now no canal-carrying

73 *Palladio in Somerset: the grand touch on a small stone warehouse at the terminus of the abandoned Westport Canal (*BW; Arthur Watts Collection*).*

that involves the use of original wharfs and warehouses. Details, buildings, even entire ports have been lost. In towns disused wharfs have been cleared to make way for car parks. Flashy supermarkets and offices are raised on the plinth where a plain-spoken warehouse stood. In villages and rural areas the sites of former canalside activity have often vanished completely. Yet in some places imaginative re-use of redundant buildings, often very fine ones, has taken place. In towns such as Newark, Leeds, Gloucester, Wigan, Great Driffield, Sowerby Bridge and Skipton, former wharfs and warehouses have been converted into offices, shops, flats, museums and marinas (**74** see **10**). Such re-use is often very successful, despite the haunting cultural contrasts: museums instead of working docks, high heels and office furniture where boots and barrows once scuffed sacks of spice and corn; air-conditioned pubs in former dust-laden basements. There are sleek cruisers moored where coal barges unloaded and rows of cars parked where goods trains grunted and

squealed between low sheds. Very occasionally there are wharfs that store road-delivered coal or sacks of grain. And from a boat there are still views to be had of gaunt, disused warehouses where a faint sense of commercial greatness lingers and where — for as long as they stand — there is that strange emotional tension that exists between buildings and water.

74 *A new use for an old warehouse at Skipton, Leeds & Liverpool Canal (*Bill Tissington*).*

5

Living accommodation

Buildings designed for accommodation often give canals a particular identity. It is an identity based on regional, local, or company traditions; and it is varied. Lock cottages present images of architectural sweetness and many survive (**75**), but they were just one of a range of building types provided for sheltering men and horses. These included cottage rows and terraces, larger houses for senior staff, warehouse and dwelling combinations, pubs, hotels, stables and canalside offices and huts.

75 *The sparse details and unforced prettiness of brick, paint and thatch: a lock cottage of c1800 on the Kennet & Avon Canal. The thatch has now been replaced by slate (*BW; Arthur Watts Collection*).*

Cottages

The most recognizable type of canal dwelling is that known generically as the 'cottage'. The custom of housing canal staff in purpose-built cottages began slowly in the late eighteenth century and lasted until the mid-twentieth century. By far the largest number of cottages were built in the early to mid nineteenth century, when commercial activity was intense and restructuring and improvements took place on many waterways. At the same time, older cottages were altered and extended, or given outbuildings and high-walled yards for extra security and privacy.

Canal workers were generally much better housed than their contemporaries in agriculture and industry. Oxford Canal records dating from the mid nineteenth century refer to a varied collection of company dwellings, including '$\frac{1}{2}$ acre of Land & a Cottage belonging to the Company' at Nellbridge Lock, a 'Cottage built 1849' at Weir Lock, a 'Carpenters Residence' at Napton Top Lock, a 'Foremans Cottage & garden & tool house' at Stretton Wharf and '3 cottages' at Thrupp which were 'occupied by the Company's Mason, Carpenter & Foreman over the length from Heyford to Oxford' in the summer of 1840.

At first glance many canal cottages look unexceptional and similar to hundreds of others in town and country. But close-up the differences emerge. They were often shaped by the special requirements of topography and were

76 *Part of the geology: a Leeds & Liverpool lock cottage of c. 1816. Sandstone walls, dressings and roof slates: as much a product of the local soil as an apple tree or a towpath hedge (*BW; Arthur Watts Collection*).*

designed to serve specific needs. At locks they were often built split-level to accommodate a sloping site. Some stand silhouetted on embankments or huddled against a lonely bridge. There were cottages built at remote reservoirs, or mounted above a tunnel mouth. Many were built on the edge of towns and were soon engulfed by factories and gasworks. Plans might include connected buildings: an office, a store-room or stable. Often a cottage was only one room deep, with windows at the front and a blind back. Unusual details included the small square or arrow-slit 'look-outs' at bedroom level, which allowed a lock-keeper to keep an eye on night traffic. There was much variety and much incidental drama. Each cottage was a landmark on the way to or from somewhere else, and the best of them displayed an organic sense of place in their use of local brick, local stone, local roofing materials and local colours (**76**).

To begin with, many canal companies did not bother with purpose-built housing. Locks were left unsupervised or attended by a part-time keeper who lived elsewhere and was probably occupied with farming all summer. The Montgomery Canal originally had no lock-keepers living on the job. The Weaver Navigation only had a few: in December 1762 the committee ordered construction of 'a small piece of building' at Acton Bridge for Thomas Dean, a lock-keeper, 'to reside in'. In the 1790s Telford recommended building cottages on the Grand Union so that lock-keepers could keep traffic moving, supervise water control and prevent damage by hurrying boatmen. On other canals the story was different. The Thames & Severn Canal Company built a series of watch-houses in the 1780s (**77**). These were of stone and were circular in plan. They look very similar to Stroud Valley wool-drying stoves. The Aire & Calder and the Calder & Hebble navigations were building more orthodox single-storey stone cottages by the late 1770s, although surviving examples, in the same style, may be of later date.

Eighteenth-century vernacular features — local materials, rustic appearance, few and simple details, plank doors, sliding sashes —

77 *A Thames & Severn watch-house: a stone tower with Gothic details and a functional plan which included a basement stable or store, living accommodation on two floors and a roof cistern for catching rain water* (R. Butler).

persisted far into the nineteenth century. Cottage plans too remained essentially the same: one, one-and-a-half or two storeys, with two rooms either side of the entry or, on a narrower front, one room behind another. On northern canals, stone was the dominant material. Tunnel-keepers' cottages were built at Marsden, on the Huddersfield Narrow, with stone walls and stone slate roofs. Roughly squared and coursed gritstone cottages were built along the Pennine stretches of the Leeds & Liverpool, and there are stone cottages at Salterhebble Locks and Elland Quay on the Calder & Hebble. At the western end of the Kennet & Avon there are four-room, single-storey cottages with hipped roofs, built of tawny Bath stone, which may have been designed by Rennie. Moving eastwards along the same canal, red-brown and grey bricks are found in the homely, half-hipped cottages of Berkshire/Wiltshire vernacular. In the south Midlands on the Grand Union are boxy cottages with chequered brick fronts and brick 'high houses' with two-and-a-half storeys and a lot of roof space — a Northamptonshire wharf speciality. There are London stock bricks in yellow and pink-brown colours on the

Regent's Canal of 1812–20. Shropshire Union cottages are of dun-coloured or orange-red Cheshire bricks. BCN cottages are drab. The Oxford Canal has an assortment of cottages in stone, brick and render. Some are eighteenth-century, others are much later. In the nineteenth century, once long-distance canal routes, and later railways, were established, building patterns began to change. Denser red and blue Midlands bricks replaced softer eighteenth-century reds. Welsh slates travelled far and wide.

Most cottages were left plain brick or stone, but some were rendered and had their outside walls painted. Whitewash produced a range of rough, fresh effects unequalled by modern glossy paints. It was good utility stuff, useful for highlighting remote cottages and for edging doors and windows in order to reflect light on dark nights and mornings. Grand Union cottages were treated in this way from the beginning. The bridge-keepers' cottages on the Gloucester & Sharpness were fashionably white to begin with. Later they were painted in Victorian railway colours; chocolate and cream. Light stone and mid-purple brown, mid or cabbage green, grey and dark stone were the painting-and-decorating colours of rustic England in the nineteenth century. Mid-purple brown was used for doors, window-frames and outbuildings; it was a serviceable colour which faded and weathered to a range of attractive pinkish-browns. Once much in evidence around wharfs and canal yards, it is not often seen anywhere today.

Despite many being built at the height of the craze for picturesque and cottage architecture, most canal cottages remained stubbornly low-key and reticent. Cheapness was the general rule and the nods at fashion were usually restricted to a few do-it-yourself details. Occasionally there were exceptions, such as the verandah-fronted cottage at Grindley Brook Locks on the Llangollen, a Regency design of a kind used in big towns like Bristol for road tollhouses (**78**). Naive borrowing of 'polite' and

78 *Telford's tricks of shape and design: a cottage at Grindley Brook on the Llangollen Canal. The giant pilasters, rounded bay and verandah create a picturesque three-dimensional effect typical of Regency turnpike and toll houses.*

pattern book motifs could create charming effects (**79**). Stort Navigation cottages had ogee-arched windows. Round arched windows with intersecting Gothic tracery became a firm favourite on Midlands canals. A small cottage at Gailey Wharf has this type of window and there are iron-framed examples (ranging in date from

79 *Lock cottage at Eyton on the Weald, Shrewsbury Canal: a grand elevation on a humble building of the 1790s. The design is visually arresting; the gratuitous semi-circles and the squashed entrance bay have a naive, classical charm (BW; Arthur Watts Collection).*

early to late nineteenth century) on other cottages and on toll-offices, warehouses and stables. On the Oxford Canal in the 1830s and 1840s, Fred Wood, the company engineer, designed a number of lock cottages and 'night houses'. Several were built with hard blue brick plinths, slate roofs and machine-made iron windows. Their detailing included bold, neo-Tudor doorways and dripmoulds.

Gothic Revival features, often used in a haphazard way, include the circular Thames & Severn watch-houses with their medieval-looking lancets and pointed doorways. The Staffs & Worcester Co. built brick round-houses: a castellated example of 1805 stands at Gailey, a picturesque whimsy which hints at company status and identity. There was an extravagant Gothic folly of a cottage at Tinsley Locks on the Sheffield & South Yorkshire Navigation, and Gothic features occur on a stone cottage in Bath, where lancet arcading sits uneasily beneath a hipped (very un-Gothic) roof. The same clash of styles is found at Oldbury Yard, where a former cottage-cum-office of *c.* 1845 sports a wall of fiercely pointed windows beneath a smugly hipped roof.

Classicism was more suited to canals. In the early nineteenth century it signalled a new attitude to things and informed the design of cottages at various stylistic levels. There were the plain, symmetrical Georgian boxes pulled from pattern books such as John Wood's of 1806. His 'warm, cheerful, and comfortable' designs for cottages with two or four rooms were typical of many built on canals like the Kennet & Avon and the Grand Union. Robert Mylne is credited as designer of the distinctive series of Greek Revival bridge-keepers' cottages on the Gloucester & Sharpness (**80**). These are similar to examples shown in books such as Joseph Gandy's *The Rural Architect* (1805) and were popular as gate lodges, turnpike toll-houses and a rather fancy kind of 'Labourer's dwelling'. A plan of one of the Gloucester & Sharpness cottages shows minimal accommodation; a 'Kitchen etc etc', 'Bedroom' and

'Cellar'. Use of a Doric portico gives these bridge-keepers' cottages a self-importance that now looks amusing. But by the early nineteenth century the portico had become a hieratic expression of authority, and its use here is entirely appropriate to England's first important ship canal. The Gloucester & Sharpness cottages are interesting for another reason — they illustrate the tendency of canal companies to build a series of 'standard cottages' along a waterway.

In April 1775, Mrs Anne Warriner was appointed lock-keeper at Witton Brook on the Weaver Navigation. She was to be paid 6s a week and was to have a house built for her 'on the usual plan' — an early instance of the standardization which later became typical on canals. Pattern books were important to this development. So too was the employment of engineers who designed and built to a programme which can still be read today. In the 1830s Telford designed a whole series of symmetrical, bay-fronted cottages, including several two-storey versions, for the Shropshire Union system (**81**). Each has an overhanging pitched roof, a tall chimneystack and a watchful, projecting bay. Telford used the same type on his toll roads and it became a very popular design. Along the south Stratford-on-Avon, an unusual series of cheap, barrel-roofed cottages appeared in 1811–13 (**82**). These were reputedly built using techniques normally applied to bridge and tunnel construction. In 1819 John Hassell made a tour of the Grand Union and noticed a number of 'white' cottages 'slated on the roofs'. These were all of a similar design, which also spilled over onto the Leicester Line, where a collection of two-up, two-down symmetrical houses with wide brimmed roofs can be found. These simple pattern-book types were built around 1815. One stands like a sentry at the top of Foxton Locks, another crouches below a bridge at the bottom. There are examples at Watford Locks and at North Kilworth and Crick wharfs. There were others from the same family along the Northampton Arm.

Twentieth-century cottages were usually built only on busy navigations or main-line systems. The Grand Union provides a fascinating cross-section of early twentieth-century working-class housing. There are cottages built (or older ones rebuilt) in the vernacular revival style current around the turn of the century: a folksy look making much use of rendered walls, steeply pitched roofs, tall chimneys, trelliswork porches and dainty gutter brackets. Sometimes

82 *Cheap, cheerful and homely: a barrel-roofed cottage of c. 1811–13 on the south Stratford-on-Avon Canal. Single storey, with attached wash-house at left. The roof is a mixture of brick, rubble and lime mortar, covered in asphalt (*R. Butler*).*

these cottages bear the date of their construction: 1912, 1914, 1916. Between the Wars, the Grand Union built more cottages as part of its big modernization. Some of these were 'boxes with lids', derived from the Ministry of Housing *Manual* of 1919. Others returned to a more vernacular style, a mixture of spec-built fashions and public housing forms typified by the 1934 'lock keepers cottage standard detail to apply to all sites subject to variations'. These crisp-looking tile-roofed cottages work surprisingly well in 1930s' set-pieces at Hatton, Knowle and Slapton Locks.

In 1858 John Hollingshead travelled the Grand Union from London to Birmingham, gathering impressions. 'Many of the lock-houses are very pretty', he wrote, and he noticed that 'in some of the most important...the keeper is seated in a little counting-house amongst his books and papers; in some of the smaller ones, rude accounts are kept in mysterious chalk signs upon the doorway or the walls'.

Sometimes a lock-keeper also collected tolls, or else a toll-clerk lived in a lockside cottage. Where this was the case, then the cottage would often have an office attached to it. Many wharf cottages had a similar arrangement. Surviving examples and plans show that the office was usually a quite separate unit, with its own door, window and hearth. Building it on to the side of a cottage, often in the same style, was a convenient and economic way of doing things: a toll clerk's or a wharfinger's time and space was divided between office, cottage and canal-side (see **11**). Surviving combinations have simple visual qualities which were often enhanced by the addition of further parts: perhaps a stable or a small barn linked by walls to form a range of connected buildings.

By the mid-nineteenth century high-walled yards were common, especially in urban areas where security was essential. From the towpath a plank door led through to a small, often oddly shaped yard paved with brick or stone, off which might be a privy, wash-house and coal store. Outbuildings might adjoin the cottage and face onto the canal, or else were tucked away at the back or at one end of the garden.

The details of daily life could be read in these humble outbuildings, few of which have survived as complete sets. Water was supplied by a well or from a stream and the wash-house with its pitched roof, chimney and sliding sash window was usually the most substantial outbuilding. By 1900 it contained a 'copper', a mangle, a zinc bath and an indoor clothes line. It also tended to be used as a store for onions, potatoes, sticks, pots, netting, old bits of rope and the lock-keeper's bicycle. The coal store was sometimes attached to the wash-house and a lean-to pigsty was often integral with the yard wall or else stood on its own. One or two pigs were kept and fed on scraps, swill and grain. Occasionally a canal worker owned a cow which was allowed to graze along the water's edge. A wooden pigeon box might be attached to a gable or convenient piece of wall. Hen runs were more temporary affairs, although canal men often took a pride in their birds: Rhode Island Reds and Light Sussex were reliable favourites. Smart-looking Leghorns, White Wyandottes (which laid pink eggs) and bow-legged, heavy-chested Indian Game were exotic extras.

Cottage gardens had their own peculiar sweetness. There was no lawn, and flowers and vegetables were mixed together; roses and sweet peas grew alongside onions and cabbages. Broad beans, runners, caulis, kale, peas and radishes were cultivated. By the late nineteenth century everyone grew potatoes: the popular Midland variety was White Elephant. Apple, plum and pear trees were common — their gnarled remains still haunt derelict canalside gardens. Herbs like thyme, parsley, peppermint, camomile, balm and rue were in daily use. When time and inclination allowed, old-fashioned flowers such as hollyhock, love-in-the-mist, rosemary, sweet briar, Michaelmas daisies and lupins were grown.

Rows, terraces and settlements

Many of the features of isolated cottages are also found where canal communities developed, at wharfs, junctions, company yards and the larger settlements of canal ports and docks. Anywhere, in fact, where boatmen (those not living on boats) or canal men lived close to the job. There are small rows of boatmen's cottages beside the Grand Union in places like Buckby, Cosgrove and Whilton. These simple two-storey brick cottages from the early nineteenth century usually have no decoration beyond a chequered brick front or a dentilled eaves course. The same thing in brick and stone can be found on the Leeds & Liverpool, where communities grew at Lathom, Burscough, Ring O'Bells and Skipton. The 1884 Canal Boats Act, which tightened regulations about overcrowding on boats, appears to have resulted in the building of a large number of boatmen's cottages at Burscough.

The small terrace or row, not always uniform in height, was the commonest form of housing, usually built by a local contractor. There are examples at the back of wharfs at Tardebigge on the Worcester & Birmingham and Honey Street on the Kennet & Avon. An early nineteenth-century canalside row on the Oxford near Thrupp is built of Oxfordshire limestone. It was originally thatched, but was reroofed in slate after a fire in 1919. The row accommodated three canal men and their families. There were vegetable plots and fruit trees in the gardens. Fresh water was drawn from a well. Later, there was a shared wash-house and a line of coal sheds was built on the canal bank around 1900 by two brothers who worked for the canal company. A less attractive terrace built of machine-made materials stands at Stanley Ferry. It was built by the Aire & Calder Co. to house their repair yard workers. It dates from the 1870s and is built of red bricks and Welsh slate which were almost certainly delivered by railway.

Ranged around Norbury Junction on the Shropshire Union is a collection of housing

83 *Spin-off development; part of the privately built Peatwood Estate wharf at Tyrley on the Shropshire Union. Separate, but spatially connected to the canal. Three cottages linked to a stable with a community room above, originally used for estate meetings, social gatherings and church services (*BW; Arthur Watts Collection*).*

which includes company-built houses, some detached (for more senior staff) but most semi-detached and dating from the mid nineteenth century to the early twentieth century. None of these buildings is especially attractive, but they are interesting because they owe their existence entirely to the development of a canal maintenance yard on this site. There was nothing here before about 1838, except a couple of bridges and a lock cottage.

Occasionally, consciously 'designed' housing was built. Tyrley Wharf on the Shropshire Union was a private wharf development by the local Peatwood Estate (**83**). Three cottages were built by 1840 and followed by additions in the 1850s. The designs are unified and visually

pleasing, in a vaguely neo-Tudor way. More affected and just as successful are the yard cottages at Bulbourne in an 1890s Old English style with different gables, tiles and half-timbering. They were designed to house men who built lock gates and iron paddle gearing in the nearby workshops.

The shape and pattern of housing at canal settlements varied, as did the kind of accommodation provided, although it was generally of a high standard. Scattered around Hillmorton Yard are brick houses dating from the late eighteenth to mid-nineteenth century. By the 1920s these included an 'Engineers House & Garden' with four bedrooms, three living rooms, kitchen and bathroom with 'Water laid on' (**84**). The engineer's office formed a separate room attached to the house. Outbuildings included a wash-house, coal-house, w.c., a greenhouse and a 'small wooden shed'. A semi-detached pair, each with three bedrooms, two living rooms and a scullery, housed the mason and carpenter. The blacksmith had a 'cottage and garden' and the toll clerk had a 'house &

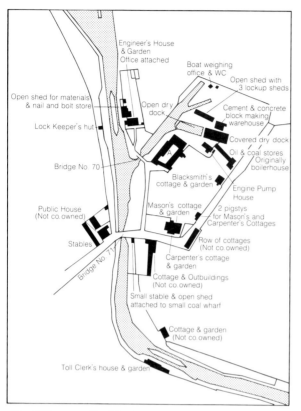

Labels in figure:
Engineer's House & Garden Office attached
Boat weighing office & WC
Open shed with 3 lockup sheds
Open shed for materials & nail and bolt store
Open dry dock
Cement & concrete block making warehouse
Lock Keeper's hut
Covered dry dock
Oil & coal stores
Originally boilerhouse
Bridge No 70
Blacksmith's cottage & garden
Engine Pump House
Mason's cottage & garden
2 pigstys for Mason's and Carpenter's Cottages
Public House (Not co. owned)
Row of cottages (Not co. owned)
Stables
Bridge No 71
Carpenter's cottage & garden
Cottage & Outbuildings (Not co. owned)
Small stable & open shed attached to small coal wharf
Cottage & garden (Not co. owned)
Toll Clerk's house & garden

84 *Hillmorton Yard in the early twentieth century: housing and maintenance buildings. The Oxford Canal Co.'s main repair shops are at A (* P. Dunn*).*

garden' next to the middle locks. There were stables, pigsties, lock-keepers' huts and, on the west side of the yard, a pub. Many of these buildings for accommodation survive, along with the workshops of the yard, creating an insular place whose residents' lives revolved around the canal which had brought them together. In the same years, at Hawkesbury Junction at the northern end of the Oxford Canal, the 'Chief Toll Clerks' very plain house consisted of five bedrooms, three living rooms, bathroom, kitchen, office, wash-house, coal-house, coach-house, outside w.c., and a 'Workman's Cottage' was provided with '2 Bedrooms, 1 Sitting Room, Kitchen & Scullery, 1 outside W.C. (flushed by culvert from the lock at stoppage time).'

Mass housing for canal workers only occurred in canal ports and docks and it was never on

the scale of that built by the railways. The Canal Age produced no Swindon or Crewe, and little in the way of company housing has survived. The Bridgewater Estate built some terraces in Runcorn, but these have been swept away. So too has most of the planned town of Goole. Goole always had the look of a frontier town, a new place with streets of uniform, red brick and slate-roofed terraces. The best of these conformed to late Georgian traditions of impressive if austere façades, with taller blocks for pubs or shops at the ends, forming vistas along Ouse, Adam and Aire streets. The workers' housing was more tightly packed and consisted of monotonous terraces, usually built on a sloping site so that they presented two storeys and a cellar to the street and three storeys to the sunken alleys which ran along the back. Rounded corners were used to good effect; they were one of Goole's hallmarks. Unfortunately, the company town was built right on top of the docks. When the docks expanded, many of the original buildings had to be demolished. A few altered, and battered fragments in Aire Street are all the original housing that remains in Goole's strange, tawdry townscape.

Ellesmere Port's original housing has suffered a similar fate, although a handful of cottages from Porter's Row, one of the earliest planned streets of the 1830s, survive as part of the Boat Museum. These humble dock-workers' dwellings were built of brick and slate by William Rigby of Runcorn and they formed a model for further housing in Union Street and Shropshire Row. There are more substantial company-built houses in Lower Mersey Street. These were built soon after 1835 for merchants' clerks and senior staff. They are not unlike the row of three-storey houses built for the Staffs & Worcester Canal Co. in Mart Street, at the north-east corner of the canal basins at Stourport. But most of Stourport's housing was built by speculators and merchants. The town grew under its own weight, rather like Shardlow, which by the mid-nineteenth century was peppered with corn merchants' houses and minor rows of canal workers' cottages.

Other groups of spin-off and canal-related housing include a mid-nineteenth century terrace at Bridgwater Dock, built overlooking the tidal basin; the curving Sunderland Terrace at Ulverston, built in connection with the ship canal, and several smaller terrace groups in Port Carlisle. These are plain, stuccoed blocks of the 1830s, some of them rubbing shoulders with what was once the Solway Hotel. In the 1870s there were great plans for Sharpness New Dock. It was to be a *grand projet*. There was to be a segment-shaped company town, with a church flanked by uniform terraces. Beyond these would be a picturesque arrangement of tree-fringed villas and grander buildings occupying the bluff towards the Old Dock. But these ambitious schemes came to nothing and Sharpness New Dock ended up with a few scattered terraces and a dreary group of houses at its east end, shoved between railway lines and water.

Wharf houses

Canal companies often provided accommodation for wharfingers and their staff of warehousemen and porters. The size and scale of the accommodation differed, but there was always a very close relation between accommodation and storage. Two main patterns existed, one being where a dwelling was combined with a warehouse, the other where it stood detached, perhaps with a connected office. The first pattern presented interesting variations. The most common was the simple tacking on of a cottage to a warehouse, as at Ripon and Tardebigge wharfs. A more unified type followed long-established farmstead patterns where a farmhouse and barn/stable/cowshed formed a longhouse range of connected buildings. This type, which occurs for example on the Oxford at Newbold and on the Kennet & Avon at Pewsey Wharf, was fairly widespread and presented a neat appearance, with everything under the same roof. The accommodation

85 *Southnet Wharf house, Leominster Canal: a simple but dignified house-cum-workplace whose rounded bay asserts authority. The basement was for storage, the rooms above for office and living accommodation (*BW; Arthur Watts Collection*).*

was either occupied by the wharfinger himself, or by his warehouseman or else both of them, as was the case in the combination, which is now a pub, at Audlem Wharf. Less common combinations included 'upside down' buildings with storage space above accommodation or vice versa. Southnet Wharf house (**85**) on the long-abandoned Leominster Canal was designed as an office and living quarters above a large storage basement. On the Thames & Severn, wharfingers inhabited a house-cum-warehouse series, each with central living quarters and symmetrical storage wings. These weird elevations looked like stage scenery and referred to Georgian polite traditions.

At many wharfs the wharfinger's house was

These buildings often appear on early nineteenth century maps as 'Navigation Offices'. Standing at the start of a canal or at a junction they were more important than a mid-line toll-clerk's cottage. Eye-catching examples stand at King's Norton Junction, at Fazeley Junction (**86**) and at Braunston stop, where the Oxford joins the Grand Union.

Contracts of employment for senior officers often included housing for the officer, his family and his horse (**87**). In 1779 the Rochdale Canal Co. built a stone house-cum-office with an attached stable for their agent Thomas Walpole. It stands overlooking the canal basins and warehouses at Sowerby Bridge. Sometimes the

86 *Reflections create unlooked-for swagger and symmetry: a 'Navigation Office' at Fazeley, where the Birmingham & Fazeley meets the Coventry Canal. This building appears on a map of 1793.*

87 *Housing for senior staff: c. 1842 plan and elevation of Horbury Bridge House, Calder & Hebble Navigation Co.*

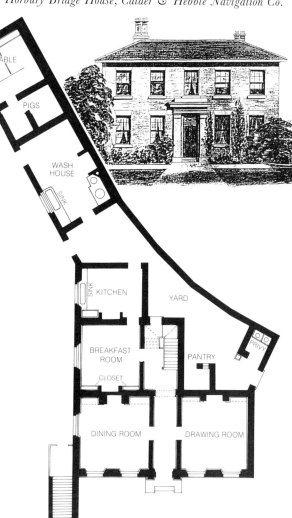

detached and faced onto a yard area, open to the canal, and flanked by warehouses, sheds and stables. Again there are similarities between this and farmstead patterns. Other layouts were more scattered, with the wharfinger's house occupying a prominent, supervisory position.

Farm life is recalled by the haphazard arrangements and the multi-use nature of wharfs, mixing living accommodation with work place and storage space. Occasionally the domestic side of a wharf interfered with its work, as in 1773, when the Calder & Hebble Navigation committee ordered, 'That no pigs or Fowls be kept at any of the Warehouses or Wharfs belonging to the proprietors'.

Larger houses

The accommodation offered to a company's senior officers could be substantial. It could also be visually arresting, especially in the case of the junction or stop houses which functioned as accommodation and administrative units where records were kept and tolls charged.

88 *Stuccoed front, brick sides; an early nineteenth century Chief Engineer's house with attached office at the self-contained, canal-orientated setting of Stoke Wharf, Worcester & Birmingham Canal* (BW; Arthur Watts Collection).

living accommodation offered to a company's top men was sumptuous, as Cobbett complained in his *Rural Rides*. On Monday 2 October, 1826, he crossed a canal near Swindon and noticed a wharf and a coal-yard and 'a gentleman's house, with coach-house, stables, walled-in garden, paddock *orne*, and the rest'. On being told that the house belonged 'to the head un o'the canal', Cobbett, who hated canals, sarcastically notes that the company's profits must be enormous for its general manager to be housed with dignity enough for a 'Secretary of State'. Most senior officers' houses were similar in size, scale and plan to the hundreds of Georgian farmhouses which graced the English countryside by the 1820s. The engineer's house at Hartshill is a good example of the type: orange-red bricks, a slate roof and a sober three-bay front looking out to the Coventry Canal. The chief engineer's house at Stoke Wharf (**88**) on the Worcester & Birmingham is a Regency box with a hipped roof

and a stuccoed front imitating ashlared stone. Its orientation is clearly towards the wharf and canal. Navigation House, which stands at one end of Northwich Repair Yard, was built in the 1850s probably for a Victorian engineer and his family. It is a plain-looking red-brown brick house, with French windows opening onto a garden and the River Weaver. Its plan incorporates an office with a doorway into the repair yard. On its entrance front is a coach-house and stable, with a stone plaque dated 1857.

The chief engineer to the Kennet & Avon lived more remotely in the white Foxhangers House at the bottom of Caen Hill Locks, but he was still close to the canal. So was Thomas Millner, northern district engineer to the Grand Junction Canal Co. at the turn of the century. Millner was a charismatic figure. He roared around on an early motorbike, took hundreds of photographs of canal work, and made his own Christmas cards showing views of Canal House, the residence he built for himself at Gayton in the 1890s. Canal House was neo-vernacular and fashionable, and the Grand Junction adopted this distinctive style for its company housing. Few canal companies how-

89 *Packet Boat Hotel, Lancaster Canal; vigorous lettering and paint used architecturally to highlight windows and quoins (*BW; Arthur Watts Collection*).*

ever could rival the panache of the Duke of Bridgewater. His large mansion built at Runcorn in the 1760s was a potent symbol of his power and authority, but he merely used it as an occasional residence during the construction of his canal.

Pubs

Temporary accommodation was offered by pubs which catered for the needs of boatmen and canal workers. Late nineteenth-century and early twentieth-century Ordnance Survey maps show hundreds along the waterways, at wharfs or junctions, in rows of cottages or at more remote spots, perhaps where a bridge took a road or a lane over a canal (see **12**). There was no hotel boom, as there was with the railways. Hotels and packet boat inns (**89**) were rare, underlining the fact that canals were mainly for freight rather than passengers.

Canal pubs were utterly simple and often

very small. They had none of the urban pub's ornamental facias, plate-glass windows or external decoration. The most basic were ordinary cottages or houses where one room, with possibly an attached taproom-cum-store, formed the pub and where the rest of the space was the publican's private quarters. Ale was fetched from a separate brewhouse which stood out the back or in an adjoining stable yard. These Georgian 'kitchen pubs' evolved an earthy, functional vernacular where the habits and needs of boatmen and canal workers were translated in visual terms into the almost-bare rooms depicted by Rowlandson around 1800. According to the reformist George Smith, a typical canal pub of the mid-nineteenth century had 'the grimiest of low-ceilinged taprooms, a truly savage and barbaric "tap" wherein is dispensed the thinnest and flattest beer'. Interiors were rough. There were floors of stone flags, bricks or sometimes boards. Walls and ceilings were just plain or whitewashed plaster. There was a large fireplace, robust furniture and untreated wood tables stained with use and spilt beer. Any decoration was accidental: a row of bottles, a jug, some odd bits of brass or pewter.

Larger canal pubs or inns (**90**) were often well-run establishments where the landlord, taking advantage of the location, often owned several small businesses. On the Leicester Line in the 1850s, the Boat Inn at Yelvertoft was run by Samuel Burrows, a 'Victualler, coal merchant and lime burner'. Not far away, Henry Dunmore sold beer from another Boat Inn and doubled up as a grazier and coal merchant. In the 1880s, John Pearson of the George Inn at Welford also dealt in coal and lime. Some landlords owned and ran boats. Most importantly, pubs had stables attached to them. These were advertised (for those who could read) by hand-painted signs on walls and gates, offering 'Stables' or 'Good Stabling' and the like. Here, for a small fee, boat horses could be fed and sheltered overnight. Country pubs usually had a meadow at the back, with a

90 *Canal pub: simple and unpretentious with paint used to good effect. The Two Boats still stands on the Grand Union Canal, but its bay windows have lost their glazing bars and the cottages to the left have gone (BW; Arthur Watts Collection).*

couple of hayricks in one corner. Town pubs kept their ricks in the stable yard. Hay was sliced off with a huge knife and forked into the horses' mangers.

Canal pubs were either privately owned or were leased by the companies. In the 1840s the 'Public House etc' at Enslow Wharf belonged to the Oxford Canal Co., as did the Anchor in Aristotle Lane, Oxford. The Leicestershire & Northamptonshire Union Canal owned Union Inn at Market Harborough Wharf, which opened in 1810. Some pubs were re-used waterside dwellings. Others sometimes doubled-up as local farm houses (**91**). Many were indistinguishable from lock or wharf cottages. A colourful sign, or the use of colour on the pub itself, or big, painted bay windows (often a later addition) gave them away.

The zealous George Smith strongly disapproved of canal pubs. He found that most had 'dirty little windows' and he was scornful of their shabby, misspelt signs advertising 'ale, porter, cider, and tobacco'. But not all pubs were dens of filth and ignorance. When the Navigation Inn at Gayton was threatened with closure in the early twentieth century, Thomas Millner championed its cause. It was, he said, 'a place where the boats make for, and many

boats stay here every night, the house supplies a special need in the District and is of very great convenience'. Unfortunately, the Navigation Inn, along with the Spotted Cow, the Crown and Anchor, the Pig and Whistle, and a thousand other honest-to-goodness canal pubs, has closed.

Hotels

In the early 1800s, Mr Colbourne, architect and assistant engineer to Ireland's Grand Canal Co., designed a chain of fine-looking hotels which started in Dublin, and ended on the Shannon. In England, canal hotels were not so common. The most impressive is the Tontine at Stourport, an E-shaped brick building with a wide front and gardens onto the Severn. The Tontine was Stourport's focal point. It functioned as a social and business centre and provided semi-permanent housing, as well as

91 *Georgic England: an unkempt field, a stable block, a faded sign: this was the Bull and Butcher, a farmhouse pub at Napton on the Oxford Canal, in 1948. With its named changed, but otherwise little altered, it is still a pub today (RCHME Crown Copyright).*

92 *The Lowther Hotel, Goole: a rectangular red brick pile built in the 1820s at the heart of the Aire & Calder docklands.*

accommodation for transient visitors and merchants. Like Stourport, Goole had its hotel. On 21 July, 1826, the *Hull Advertiser* noted that a 'large and commodious Inn, called the Banks Arms Hotel, is already opened, and fitted up in capital style'. Renamed the Lowther (**92**), the hotel still stands in a seedy dockside area, hemmed by water-filled basins and warehouses. It takes the form of a big 1820s town house and its main reception rooms are decorated with nautical motifs and scenes which celebrate the Aire & Calder achievement. In the 1830s, the Weaver Navigation built the Weaver Hotel, Runcorn, and at the new Port Carlisle the Solway Hotel opened. Despite its dour appearance the Solway catered for well-off passengers, as did the packet house hotels or inns which offered rest and refreshment to short-haul travellers, and were built at various places, especially on the Lancaster and Leeds & Liverpool. In 1851, Queen Victoria alighted at the black-and-white Packet House at Worsley on the Bridgewater Canal. She had travelled there by boat, a splendid occasion spoilt only by one of the towing horses bolting into the canal.

Stables

Until the widespread use of powered boats in the early twentieth century, horses were vital to canals. They needed a lot of looking after and many stables were built along the waterways. All stables, even the smallest, were serv-

iced, and boatmen usually paid to feed and overnight their horses. Most stables were company-owned and stood at wharfs, docks, maintenance yards, lock flights and long summits. Others were built by private business: by industrialists, wharfingers, breweries, and carrying companies. Pickford's wharfs generally had well-designed stables and Fellows, Morton & Clayton built their own. On the BCN the benevolent Incorporated Seamen and Boatmen's Friend Society provided a string of free stables at busy lock flights like Walsall, Riders Green and Rushall.

Eighteenth-century stables were often open-sided, thatched shelter sheds or hovels, a type favoured on river navigations: on the Thames flimsy, turf-roofed hovels survived until the end of the nineteenth century. On canals, early brick stables and sheds were usually cramped and filthy, especially on sluggish agricultural waterways. In the early nineteenth century, byelaws and company regulations, combined with the pressures of organized trade, imposed higher standards and most surviving stables date from this time onwards. Canal stables differed little from farm stables and to begin with they reflected the regional vernacular: timber-framed and weatherboarded with plain tiles or pantiles; brick with plain tiles or slates; stone with stone slates. Their external appearance was straightforward.

A typical stable consisted of four walls and a pitched roof. At the front was a central doorway with a door of two separately hung halves. On either side was a window. There might be a hay-loft reached by outside steps or an inside ladder, but often the stalls were open to the rafters. Soundly designed stables had 8ft high (2.5m) front walls and were well ventilated, with hopper type windows or wooden grilles to prevent draughts. Small stables had monopitch roofs and stalls along the rear wall. Often there was room for only two horses. Outside there was a manure pit or a tiny walled midden. Inside a stable, the floor was surfaced with brick pavers or cobbles and drained into a channel either in the centre or at the rear. There were individual stalls for the horses, separated from one another by partitions which were sloped and stoutly boarded to prevent horses kicking or biting one another (**93**). Each stall had a tethering ring, a wall-mounted hayrack of wood or iron, and a manger into which oats, chaff and mangel mixes were ladled. Oats and chaff were stored in rat-proof wooden bins (or delivered as needed) and were laced with confetti to discourage pilfering. Hay was kept in a loft or in a netted bay at one end of the building. Water was simply drawn by bucket out of the canal, horses being lovers of pond water.

The Leeds & Liverpool and the Lancaster were well supplied with stables; the Lancaster built a whole series between Kendal and Preston. Along the Shropshire Union, where the company did most of the carrying, there are stables which vary in size from small brick blocks for four horses to larger examples at Audlem and at Bunbury Locks. The Bunbury example, which is similar to railway type stables, had stalls for 22 horses and a forage store. It stands right on the lockside, its doors opening straight onto the towpath in a common and economical layout which meant that tow-ropes could be untied and horses led straight inside. The same proximity to the canal is found at two mid-nineteenth-century blocks; one at Delph Locks on the Dudley Canal, the other, in derelict state, on the Middlewich Branch. Both of these are built to a similar design. The Middlewich one stands close to a contemporary canal cottage, once occupied by a horse-keeper. There are small stable blocks still standing at the top and the bottom of Foxton Locks and in the 1930s the Grand Union built a series of simple, clean-looking stables as part of their improvement programme. As late as the 1960s, a horse was stabled at Northampton Top Lock to help unpowered butties up the flight.

At wharfs the orientation of stables to water differed. Gayton on the Grand Union and

93 *Interior of a boat-horse stable of the 1870s, Burnley Wharf, Leeds & Liverpool Canal. Stone setts, wooden partitions, cast-iron posts with 'boskins'; king-post roof trusses. This stable and its equipment still survive (P. Dunn).*

Marston Doles on the Oxford each had a stable range at the back of the site, forming one side of an enclosed yard area; a fairly typical arrangement. At other wharfs stables were built obliquely, for no obvious reason, or set at right angles to the canal. Stables were often combined with other buildings: in the 1840s the Oxford Canal chain book records 'Stables with large store room over' at Clifton Wharf and 'Stables for 4 horses with a boathouse over' at Rugby Wharf. The largest canal-related stables stood on the BCN: fortlike brick blocks with stalls on two levels, built by nineteenth-century railway companies with canal interests. These had a permanent staff of horse-keepers and were open round the clock. After dark they were atmospheric places: lantern light glimmered on collars and harnesses hung up on wooden pegs, and giant shadows flitted across rafters. At the other end of the scale were the hackney boxes (with room for a pony and trap) which accompanied houses built for a company's senior officers. And at private farm wharfs or at lock cottages there were very small stables, lean-tos and narrow brick sheds with a hay loft above two stalls. At Stretton Stop, on the Oxford, a small stable was combined with a tool shed.

Toll offices and huts

Offices, huts and sheds served a variety of purposes on canals. The most interesting small offices were those built for toll clerks at minor junctions or at intermediate points. Toll-collecting was an important job. At a toll office a boat was stopped so that the clerk could inspect its cargo, measure its freeboard with a gauging rod and check its tonnage against an index kept in the office. If all was in order, a prescribed toll was paid and the boat went on; if not, an extra toll was charged. Toll clerks might work from the front room of a cottage, from an office attached to a cottage, or from a free-standing building. Among the latter, the most eye-catching were the octagonal toll offices once widespread on Midlands canals. There was a series on the Staffs & Worcester, with round arched, iron-framed windows and slate roofs. A slender one still commands Bratch Locks, whilst a squatter example survives at Stewponey Wharf. Telford made a neat design drawing of a similar 'Ticket Office' for his Birmingham New Main Line (**94**). The type was very common

94 *Telford's design for a 'Ticket Office' on the BCN (Redrawn by P. Dunn from an original in the archives of the Institution of Civil Engineers).*

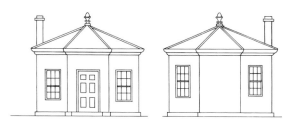

95 *Aire & Calder toll office, Stanley Ferry. A self important design of 1829; the Doric style refers to the great aqueduct nearby (*BW; Arthur Watts Collection*).*

on the BCN: preferred locations were next to bridges or locks, or on purpose-built islands in the middle of the waterway. These gauging or indexing stations were linked to the towpath by a swivel plank across the narrows.

Other free-standing toll offices took the form of plain brick boxes with tiled or slated roofs, like the example at Great Haywood, which is enlivened by the favoured Gothic traceried windows. The unobtrusive office at Gailey Wharf is not untypical of many that have vanished. Late toll offices tend to be fussy by comparison with early ones. Examples include the Aire & Calder office at Stanley Ferry, a charming 1830s' Doric pavilion (**95**), and the York Street office in Stourport, which is inscribed with the date 1853. There is an assertive little building at Brentford Locks and a summerhouse-like toll office at Norton Junction with a large bay window. Small offices like this continued to be built or replaced in the twentieth century until nationalization made the whole concept of toll-collecting redundant.

The interior of a toll office was spartan. It consisted of one room, with limewashed walls and a window or two, and sometimes a hatch for passing tickets and money through. There was a fireplace or a stove, a desk with a high stool and a shelf or a small cupboard to hold ledgers and paperwork. In one corner was a gauging rod or two, and there was the usual collection of odds and ends: company regulations pinned to the wall, a lantern and candles, a coal bucket, hand-painted signs and a chain to stretch across the narrows in emergencies. In remote offices, a toll-clerk was sometimes supplied with a gun, usually a blunderbuss, to frighten thieves away.

At the lowest end of the accommodation scale were huts provided to shelter working lock-keepers, leggers, lengthsmen and reservoir-keepers (**96**). Many of these still stand in various states of decay. They were typically no bigger than a potting-shed — just four walls, often with no window, a roof, a fireplace and a plank door. In the Midlands they are still called 'hovels' or 'lobbies'. Some rough, stone-built huts on the Avon Navigation may be eighteenth century. Common examples from the nineteenth century are built of brick with pitched slate roofs and, from the twentieth century, of brick with monopitch concrete roofs.

Local specialities include the circular, domed lobbies on the old Chester Canal (now the Shropshire Union) which are early and rather stylish (**97**). They belong to the same family as well-houses, valve houses and village lock-ups. On the Grand Union there are reservoir-keepers' huts built entirely of brick, with barrel-vaulted, tarred roofs. Telford, for whom no problem was too small, designed tiny huts for his BCN New Main Line; one type was intended to fit snugly into the curling wall of a roving bridge. In the BCN canyons leading away from Cambrian Wharf there are unexpected survivals: brick sheds built against factory walls. Some have the round arched Gothic window, which looks strange and delicate in such a setting. In railway days 'lineside huts' began to appear. On GWR-owned canals there are rickety, sleeper-built huts, each with a felt roof and a brick stack at the rear. Prefabricated concrete post-and-panel sheds are another railway legacy.

A lock-keeper's hut was his bolt hole and base. He kept the tools of his trade — a long-handled rake or 'drag' and a three-pronged 'ice-podger' — slung under its eaves. His hours

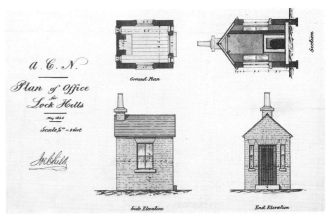

96 *Attention to detail: an 1865 design for a lock-keeper's office on the Aire & Calder (*BW Archives*).*

were often cold and lonely, especially after dark in the winter. On the Oxford as late as the 1950s, two shifts of lock-keepers worked on the Napton flight, from 5am to 1pm and from 1pm to 9pm on weekdays. Huts like that at Napton Top Lock were somewhere to shelter from the rain, get a fire going and cook some breakfast.

97 *A lock lobby on the old Chester Canal (now the Shropshire Union) which was constructed in the 1770s. A sturdy, characterful building of brick with a heavily moulded stone cornice (*BW; Arthur Watts Collection*).*

6

Life on the cut

To travel by canal boat is to make a journey. At three or four miles per hour, distances stretch out and are measured in days: Birmingham once more seems a long way from London. The feeling of being pleasantly drawn along and enveloped by the corridor of water is strong. And with it come occasional glimpses of the working boatman's world, his line of life which wound across the country with its own peculiar scenery and accessories, its own habits and traditions. Some of the fabric of that old canal world remains. Its tightly-drawn spaces — small cabins, narrow locks, low bridges, cramped tunnels — can still be experienced. Its homely landscapes of tilled fields and hedgerows, of factories and industry, of village wharfs and shadowing railways partly survives today. There are still isolated locks and bridges lining up through drowsy acres of corn. Here and there are cottage gardens stuffed with vegetables, or warehouses with slate roofs that glint dully in the rain. There are thousands of anecdotes, engravings, photographs and even film footage of the Canal Age. But despite these survivals, it takes imagination to reconstruct the human histories, the lost buildings, the endless numbing journeys and pungent flavour of working days on England's waterways (**98**).

'Their Habits and their whole Lives are detached as it were from those around them', the Reverend John Davies reported of the canal boatmen in 1841. To a boat family 'the cut' was not a backdrop but the whole of their lives.

They lived on it, moved on it and reacted to it: they were part of its fabric. And interwoven with the architectural forms of engineering and commerce were other, less common building types, made to serve the needs of the working boatman. Churches, chapels, missions and schools provided for his spiritual and educational welfare. Boatyards, ranging from small, private premises to highly organized company docks and carrying fleet bases, supplied and maintained his boat. Well-observed contrasts were formed between the static architecture of canals and the mobile architecture of boats in all sizes, shapes and colours, each designed to fit its own particular waterways.

Boats

Along Britain's coasts and estuaries sailed hoys, sloops, coasters, scheovers and yarms. Up and down its rivers crawled clinker-built Severn trows, Weaver and Mersey flats, East Anglian wherries, Fen lighters, Thames and Medway barges, fat-bellied Humber keels and sloops, Billy-boys, Wey barges, Scows and Puffers. Boats with red sails stood silhouetted against the flat countryside of Norfolk, the vale of York and the Humber. There was a rich regional diversity of traditional wooden craft some of which, such as the Yorkshire keels, had ancient origins.

Canals developed their own specialized craft. There were barges. There were wide or short boats on broad canals like the Bridgewater, the

98 *Factories, 'floating cottages', and washing idling in the breeze: the homely and the un-homely in sharp juxtaposition. A scene on the Grand Union Canal in working days (*BW Archives*).*

Leeds & Liverpool and the Lancaster. On some canals, rakish-looking packet or 'swift' boats plied, carrying fare-paying passengers in a saloon panelled like a Georgian dining room. In the 1830s, an excellent timetabled service was provided on the Lancaster Canal between Kendal and Preston, with two horses pulling the packet at a cracking 10 miles (16km) per hour. Horses were changed at regularly spaced stables and at Lancaster a packet boathouse was built for maintenance. Similar packet routes operated on the Bridgewater, the Kennet & Avon, and the Regent's Canal, where an often rowdy service was lampooned by Rowlandson. In South Wales there were double-prowed open

boats. On hilly West Country and Shropshire canals there were tub-boats, floating boxes which banged their way through locks and crawled over intriguing inclined planes.

The most famous type of craft developed for canal use was the narrow boat. This was an English design of unique and eccentric dimensions: 70ft long and 7ft wide (21 × 2m), a low, black shape, usually with a cabin at the back. Dangerous on swollen rivers or estuaries and definitely unsuitable for putting to sea, narrow boats were inland craft whose heartland was the Midland canal maze. Within the type, which included BCN Joeys or day boats, family boats and lithe-looking 'fly' boats, there were endless permutations. Canal companies and boatyards built with their own styles and purposes in mind. 'Barlow boats' and 'Ricky boats' were named after boatyard firms. Fellows, Morton & Clayton boats were generally reckoned to be the smartest. In the 1930s, the Grand Union Canal Co. produced narrow boats with differing specifications: the Star, Town, or Royalty classes.

The inventor of the English narrow boat is unknown, but its origins must date back to the 1760s, when the decision was taken to construct the Pioneering Trent & Mersey with locks that measured roughly 72ft by 7ft 6in. Long, narrow boats were made to fit exactly into long, narrow locks. They were cheap to build and used up little water in relation to their carrying capacity. Most narrow boats had open holds suitable for shovelling in coal, grain, lime or sand and stone. Once loaded, the cargo could be protected by side-cloths. Short-haul types like the BCN Joeys were double-ended; simple geometrical boats that could work both ways. Joeys usually had no cabin, but long-distance narrow boats did and this cabin was a tiny miracle of spatial organization; 'the smallest

*99 The smallest home imaginable: a narrow-boat cabin at Stoke Bruerne Museum (*BW Archives*).*

place of its kind in the whole world' according to one Victorian journalist. It was a place which might be home to a family of four or five people (**99**).

A typical narrow boat cabin was a framed and planked wooden box, perhaps 10ft long and 5–6ft wide (3 × 2m). Inside, everything was within hand's reach. Fitted around a cabin's walls were lockers and panelled drawers and cupboards, a small bottle stove or cooking range which was kept almost permanently lit, a hinged table-cupboard and a foldaway bed. A side bed opposite the range doubled up as a bench. To look through the back doors of a late nineteenth century cabin was to look into a colourful shrine of personal effects, knick-knacks and painted decoration. The Victorian fad for cramming ornaments into living rooms found expression here, in the winking brass knobs, lace-edged plates, lacework curtains, polished lock keys, Measham teapot and gleaming oil lamp. At the back of the cabin near the doors was a 'soap 'ole' and a ticket drawer for keeping toll tickets, sweets, tobacco, matches and other odd items. Food was kept in the pantry beneath the stern deck. Cabins were fairly standard in layout and equipment, and their ingenious space-and-labour saving design appears to have altered little over a hundred years or so of narrow boat building.

Boatyards

Boats were built in boatyards or boatdocks. River navigation yards were ramshackle places occupying a flat slice of bank. Typically they consisted of a rudimentary slipway, a timber stack, a sawpit and a patchwork of wooden sheds often cobbled together from broken doors and old deck timbers. Boats were built in the open and the work was similar, especially with keeled craft, to ship building (**100**). When finished, boats were launched sideways or end on into the water. Canal yards were very similar, although some developed a less temporary appearance and others were quite large and formed part of an inland port or settlement

100 *The timeless way of barge building: hewn, sawn and bent timbers propped and sheltered beneath canvas on a bank of the Basingstoke Canal, 1932 (*BW Archives*).*

like Stourport, Braunston and Shardlow. At Worsley, the Duke of Bridgewater's yard employed over 100 men building and repairing boats nicknamed 'dukers' and 'starvationers', the special, lean-looking craft which worked in the canal tunnels of Worsley mines.

On the BCN hundreds of boatyards maintained thousands of boats. There were many independent yards scattered across the system. Most were family businesses employing six to twelve men including apprentices, a blacksmith, a boat-painter and boat-builders. Each yard had its own style and traditions and despite obvious similarities, no two narrow boats were ever identical. Boats were supplied for different kinds of customers; the famous Nurser's Yard at Braunston (established in the 1870s) built for well-known carriers like Fellows, Morton & Clayton, and Samuel Barlow, as well as for the occasional owner-boatman. With eight men on the job it took about six weeks to build a horse-powered narrow boat. It was thorough, manly work using steam

bent planks and wooden joints and pegs. Maintenance work, the bread-and-butter of small yards, consisted of caulking (thumping oiled oakum between planks to seal them) tarring hulls, painting and decorating, carpentry repairs and chalicoing. Chalico was a potent mix of 'hoss muck', tallow and tar. Smelling memorably, it was heated in a chalico boiler and applied hot, with a paper backing, to the side planks inside a narrow boat.

Small yards that built only a handful of wooden boats a year tended to diversify. Some repaired and painted farm carts. Others sold coal or canvas. Boatyards serving river systems made ropes and sails as well as river and canal craft. Harry Fletcher's book *A Life on the Humber* recalls Dunston's keel-yard and its sail-loft, 'a light, airy room above the stairs, smelling of tarry twine and the beeswax used to soften the twine for sewing'. The loft was reached by outside steps and was lit by long windows. Dunston's seemed to make everything and the sights, sounds, and smells of a working boatyard were fascinating. There was a constant noise of sawing and hammering which echoed around tumble-down workshops and makeshift sheds. Half-finished boats lay at odd angles. There

101 *Disorder and improvisation: a Midlands boatyard in c. 1900, occupying a sliver of bank between the water and a hedge (BW Archives).*

102 *Plan of Bull's Bridge Yard; the Grand Union's large, highly-organised carrying fleet depot in the mid-twentieth century (P. Dunn).*

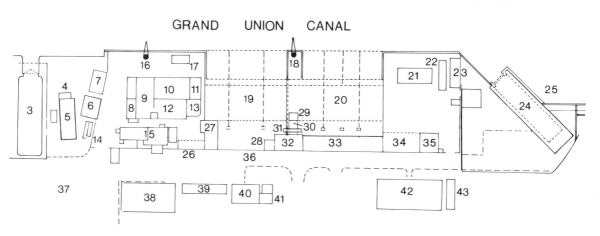

1 Bulls Bridge	12 Machine Shop	23 Oil Store	34 Timber Store
2 Towing Path	13 Men's Cloaks	24 Paint Dock	35 Paint Shop
3 Dry Dock	14 Toilets	25 Mooring Layby	36 Roadway
4 Kitchen	15 Office Block	26 Cycles	37 Roadway
5 Canteen	16 No. 1 Crane 30 cwt	27 Blacksmith's Shop	38 No. 1 Stores
6 Electrician	17 Fuel Tank	28 Men's Cloaks	39 Coke Store
7 Degreasing Shop	18 No. 2 Crane 5 cwt	29 Office	40 Salvage & Plant
8 Women's WC/Toilet	19 No. 1 slipway	30 Boiler House	Maintenance
9 Engine Maintenance Shop	20 No. 2 slipway	31 Steam Box	41 Welding Shop
10 Engine Overhaul Shop	21 No. 2 store	32 Carpenters Shop	42 Sailmakers
11 Test	22 Fuel Tank	33 Saw Mill	43 Fuel Tank

were open stacks of seasoning timber, a steam box for bending planks and rusty windlasses for hauling boats out of the water. The whole place was scented with wood-shavings and littered with tar pots, ropes, trestles and staging, broken tillers, rudders and bits of old iron-mongery. Nothing was every thrown away and no money was ever spent at a boatyard (**101**).

Layouts varied. Larger boatyards were similar to maintenance yards, although their range of activities was not so great. Smaller yards only needed a narrow water frontage. Taylor's in Chester and Tooley's in Banbury are typical canal boatyards. Taylor's dates from the mid to late nineteenth century and includes an open-sided boat-building shed with iron pillars supporting a slate roof. This is right on the waterfront. Beyond it stands a Cheshire flat-builder's shed. At the back of the site is a brick smithy with a slate roof, a weatherboarded carpenter's shop and a stable block. The large boat-building shed is a late example of a type which at the lower end of the scale meant a tin shack on wheels which could be rolled over a boat so that work could proceed in wet weather. Tooley's Yard is a rare survivor which dates back to the 1790s and is still used for boat repair today (see **13**). The site is cramped, triangular and authentically messy. Here boats were built on a wedge-shaped space right at the canal's edge, and launching was a sideways push into the water. Behind this boat-building space lies the 90ft (27m) long brick-lined dry dock, angled to the canal. This was originally open and was given its corrugated-iron covering by George Tooley earlier this century. Here boats were repaired. Beyond the dry dock the yard ends abruptly with a line of down-at-heel workshops and an original blacksmith's shop. This low-scaled smithy is not unlike the Taylor's example, although here the roof is of plain tiles.

The biggest boatyards were early twentieth-century and were virtually communities in their own right. Bull's Bridge Repair Yard (**102**), which continued in operation until the 1990s is a good example. This yard was created in

103 *The Paint Shop at Bull's Bridge in the mid-twentieth century: timber-framed, clad in corrugated iron and heated by a floor-mounted stove. Standard issue equipment — lamps, wooden tillers, Buckby cans and so on — was painted up in here (*BW Archives*).*

the 1930s to serve the newly formed Grand Union carrying fleet. In the 1940s and '50s, it expanded into a complex of tough-looking steel-framed and metal-clad buildings with several acres of concrete flooring. It was an unlovely but bustling place with its giant boat lay-by, yawning slipways and echoing workshops. At the height of its activity it was the largest canal boat depot in Britain, employing up to eighty staff and providing an unequalled service including everything from major rebuilding and engine overhauls to manufacturing specialized parts and making wooden patterns, lamps, water-cans, tip-cat fenders, side-cloths and mops (**103**). Traditional boatyard staff such as carpenters, painters, sailmakers, blacksmiths and boatbuilders worked at Bull's Bridge. Modern trades were covered by mechanics and fitters, electricians and welders. It must have been exciting, even in post-war years, for a young apprentice, to work in the shallow paint dock or the galleried parts store, with its lockers and racks full of boat equipment. After commercial carrying ceased, Bull's Bridge turned out holiday boats. Its final years were

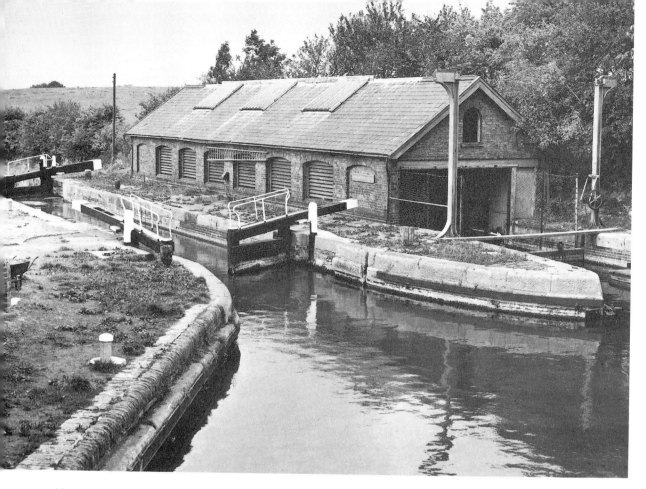

104 *Dry dock at Marsworth Locks, Grand Union Canal: stock bricks, slate roof, slatted openings. Dry docks were often built alongside locks so that they could fill and drain easily (*Derek Pratt, Waterways Photo Library*).*

spent building and repairing British Waterways' tugs and maintenance craft.

A useful repair facility at a boatyard was a dry dock. The dry dock at Tooley's Yard is typical of many that were built alongside canals, especially in the nineteenth century. Usually, these brick (or stone) lined and paved chambers are only big enough to take one boat at a time. They are rectangular and have a rounded or squared end, with drop-planks or a gate at the entry. Often sited on their own, with no covering or ancillary buildings, their detail is usually minimal. They performed the job of allowing boats to be floated in, the water drained and repairs carried out. Early dry docks, like early river navigation locks, were

cheaply built turf-sided structures and no examples survive. Later brick or stone examples are to be found at boatyards, some maintenance yards and occasionally at wharfs or canal junctions. Covered dry docks occur on the Grand Union at Braunston Marina (formerly Nurser's Boatyard) and at Braunston Bottom Lock — a hipped roof building of *c.* 1816 lit by a range of large windows. This building was company owned and doubled up as a weigh dock, where the cargo-carrying capacity of boats was gauged for toll purposes. The smart white-brick, slate-roofed dry dock opposite the Wendover Arm junction (**104**) is another Grand Union example, with details which bear a stylistic resemblance to the nearby Bulbourne Yard. Open-sided or verandah-type examples include Dutton Dock on the Trent & Mersey. This may date from the 1770s, but in the late nineteenth century, under railway ownership, it acquired a blue brick store-room and a roof

105 *Dutton dry dock, Trent & Mersey Canal: eighteenth-century origins, nineteenth-century railway style. The valanced wooden canopy on cast-iron pillars and the blue brick store at the back of the dock were built by the LNWR (*Alastair Marshall*).*

with a valanced canopy (**105**). A larger covered dock stands on an island site opposite Taylor's Boatyard in Chester. This is oval-ended with stepped, sandstone walls and a brick paved floor. Its hipped slate roof is iron-framed and carried on iron pillars.

At places like Gloucester, Stourport and Stone, dry docks form part of larger canal complexes. Two wet and two dry docks line the waterfront of Stone Boatyard. At Stourport, where boatbuilding flourished from the 1770s onwards, open and covered docks, entered from the basins, allowed narrow boats and river barges to be repaired. Two dry docks are still in use — one beneath a modern agricultural canopy alongside the narrow locks, and another in the boatyard in Upper Basin, hidden inside a corrugated iron shed.

Dry-dock design changed little over the years. The Paint Dock built at Bull's Bridge in the 1940s was brick-lined and had wooden gates just like late eighteenth-century examples. Boats were floated in, and as the dock drained through a sluice leading to a local stream, their flat bottoms settled onto low brick walls running across the floor.

Painted boats (106)

Roses, castles, sailing boats, mountains, a sunset over a lake, a hump-backed bridge: the mixture of architecture and fantasy is a strange one. The image of coloured boats forming a contrast with rough cargoes and hard, undecorated lives is poignant. The origins of the tradition of painting boats in this way are not clear. It probably had much to do with nineteenth-century folk-art and the working-class habit of decorating gypsy caravans, farm carts and fairground equipment. Between 1800 and 1850 there was a fashion for gaudy papier-mâché trays, glass paintings, encrusted grandfather clocks and cheap furniture. That perhaps accounts for the all-over decoration, although on boats this was restricted to certain parts.

107

106 *Painted boat: the cabin of S. Barlow's 'Rosie Agnes' in 1948. Roses, an icon-like castle, geometrical patterns and extra-bold lettering, with the name swimming along the top bend* (BW Archives).

What is clear is that in being highly decorative canal boats were not unique. What is unique is the kind of decoration they were given.

Ruined castles and mountains are romantic scenes which stem from the Gothic Revival and English Picturesque traditions. Mixed in with these are more homely images: roses (which the Victorians loved) seen in hedges and cottage gardens, floral patterns remembered from Staffordshire coffee-pots. The fantasy towers standing next to what look like ordinary canal bridges were visible along the Thames & Severn and the Staffs & Worcester. And those panels painted with turrets and Shangri-La sunsets refer to the fact that 'an Englishman's home is his castle', even one which floats amidst the muck and smoke of the cut (see **14**). Beyond this there is the ancient maritime tradition of decorating boats: the English men o' war at Trafalgar had painted figureheads and gilded sterns.

Not all waterway craft were highly decorated — it would have been inappropriate for filthy colliery boats. Short-haul BCN boats had simple fore-end decorations of coloured circles, crescents and diamonds, often incorporating a company name and trademark: Johnson's Iron & Steel Ltd had an eye painted on the fore-end of their boats; a strange, Homeric device. Thames barges had curly scroll-work on their transoms, Leeds & Liverpool short boats displayed 'liquorice allsorts' patterning along their top bends. But it was on long-distance narrow boats that the outbursts of roses, castles and lettering were seen at their best, turning a boat into a colourful piece of travelling theatre.

There were endless varieties of painted boats. Each major yard or company had its own emblems and colours. Painters had their own styles. Like the building of standard bridges, the painting of similar subjects — roses, castles, scrolls, geometrical shapes — presented thousands of images without any two being exactly alike. Typically, a narrow boat's hull was black (painted with coal tar to protect it) with white or straw lining-out. Prow and stern details might be scarlet and blue. The real blaze of colour came with the cabin. Here vivid lettering was interspersed with red and yellow roses and green leaves. There were icon-like panels on the cabin doors depicting Bohemian castles or other scenery. Sliding hatches often had a large heart or an ace of clubs painted on them. The cabin top might be diamond patterned. Tillers were as gaily striped as maypoles, and the boat's name was carved or painted, often in raking letters, along the top bends.

Favourite colours were azure blue, dark royal blue, chrome yellow, vermilion red, pink, light brown, and dark and middle green. Using hand-ground flat paints, a skilful painter worked easily, almost casually. He knew the right use of light colours against dark, the right way to block in lettering, the best space to fill with a floral bouquet. Once dry, the paintwork was varnished to make it shine. It never peeled, it just gently faded and occasionally needed touching up or re-doing.

Boatyards usually had their own painters and much of their earlier twentieth-century work is well recorded. Herbert Tooley's roses were succulent and famous. Harry Taylor and his son were past masters, producing flamboyant lettering and real-looking castles inspired perhaps by Chirk Castle or the King Charles Tower in Chester. In the 1930s and '40s, Frank Nurser painted highly characteristic daisies as well as roses, dogs' heads, horses' heads and castles. His apprentice Percy Foster managed some inspired paintwork. Bill Hodgson worked for the Anderton Co., specializing in mountain sunsets and branching out into sailors' heads and village and farmyard scenes. In the 1920s Harry Atkins ran Polesworth Yard on the Coventry and did all the signwriting. His son Isaiah painted castles that looked like exploding fireworks. There were others: George Preston at Saltley, Harry Crook at Uxbridge, Frank Jones of Leighton Buzzard and Tom Ditton who worked at Bull's Bridge from 1936 to 1957.

Much boatyard painting meant company liveries and lettering. Early on, Pickford's fast fly-boats were identified with a large diamond painted on their sides. Rochdale Canal Co. flats were liveried in red, white and blue. Salt Union boats had black cabins with yellow lettering. Lettering was important and much space was given to advertising carrying company names and bases. Registration details were less prominent: their display was merely a legal requirement. Straightforward English block and sans serif, brash egyptian and grotesque derivatives or the more flowery penformed lettering were popular on canals and formed much of the day-to-day work for yard and dock painters.

Careful thought was given to the choosing and painting of a boat's name. Old narrow boats had jolly, earthy names, not perhaps as suggestive as those of early railway locomotives, but often just as misspelt. Amongst other things inspiration came from animals, birds, legendary beasts, mortals, demi-gods, gods and goddesses, towns, flowers, stars and girls. There were boats called Pansy, Bramble, Chub, Dolphin, Elaine, Kate, Jane, Angela, Saturn (a popular one), Nimrod, Nautilus, Duchess–Countess, Rose of Sharon, Golden Spray and the deliciously named Flower of Gloster.

Boatmen (107)

In 1880 George Smith made a voyage from London to Leicester which he later described in *Canal Adventures by Moonlight*. Smith was a reformer and a fact-finder. He estimated that the horse towing his boat had plodded some 80,000 miles (129,000km) in 12 years or so of service. Towards Leicester he found 'deep and tumble-down' locks, slummy working boats whose crews looked like scarecrows and 'lots of swearing women and children'. Appalled at the 'evils' he found on his inland tour, Smith lobbied for action which resulted in the Canal Boats Acts of 1877 and 1884. These Acts raised the profile of canals in general and went some way to cleaning up living conditions and regulating life on boats. But what was life on a working boat like? By the late nineteenth

107 *Boat horse and boatman, c. 1920s. The powerful-looking horse wears full harness with a collar and side ropes with bobbins. The boatman is dressed in gaberdine* (BW Archives).

century canals were drawing the attention of philanthropists as well as artists and journalists in search of a good story. It had much to do with a canal's strange mixture of practicality and romance — coal-laden holds and painted cabins — and with the secretive, close-knit community of its boat families and their unusual lifestyle.

The origins of canal boatmen may never be properly understood. But a newly completed canal had to attract new users — boatmen as well as customers. The sudden appearance of boatmen and then small populations of boat families undoubtedly gave rise to the persistent idea that they were gypsies who had taken to the water. Their dark, weathered appearance was confirmation enough. 'It ain't the sun', Temple Thurston was told in *The Flower of Gloster* that gave boatmen that 'dark hair, dark eyes, that browny sort of skin...'. It was in their blood. In fact the Romany links are at best tenuous. It was the rootless existence of the canal families with their horses and wooden boats that gave rise to the 'water gypsy' myth.

Most boats appear to have been owned by businessmen — iron founders, colliery owners, lime-merchants, manufacturers and transport firms such as Pickford's. Later, independent carrying companies emerged and publicans, wharfingers and farmers sometimes owned smaller numbers of boats. Occasionally there were owner-boatmen but there were never many and the 'Number One', as he was called, has proved to be something of an elusive figure. The men who worked the boats came (like most people joining the Industrial Revolution) off the land where they had been peasant farmers or perhaps local carriers. Where a canal ran close to a river or the coast they may have transferred from one kind of waterway to another. To begin with boatmen lived 'on the land' in towns or villages. If they had to make overnight journeys they stayed in pubs or slept in the boat's hold. In the Black Country, many boatmen worked by day and went home at night throughout the Canal Age. Exactly when families began to live and work entirely on boats is not clear, but it must coincide with the opening of through-routes and the increasing need for industries to send and receive long-distance cargoes. The idea that railway competition forced families to leave their homes and take to living on boats has been revised: people were living on working boats before the railways came. Once established, the tradition remained unbroken — the same family names occur on the Grand Union in the 1860s as in the 1960s.

Boatmen lived with a horizon that was always slowly moving. They lived with the weather and the seasons. In winter their narrow world drew itself even tighter as horses slithered on miry towpaths, frozen ropes corkscrewed over lock beams and the canal iced up. On twilit afternoons the helmsman's view was reduced to basic elements — earth, air and water; the monotony of empty fields and hedges relieved only by the occasional farm or lamplit wharf. A boatman's route knowledge was excellent. He would keep going on the darkest night and in fog that was so thick the front of the boat vanished. One old boatman described the 20-mile (32km) Leicester Line summit as 'a hell of ice in winter' and 'a bower of wild roses in June'. In summer the repetitive journeys were easier. Locks shimmered in the haze and heat bounced off the cabin roof. Oaks and elms billowed along the towpath. In summer too the boatmen were often blamed for poaching and

petty theft. A mid-nineteenth-century account of their general dishonesty included accusations of cutting grass and mowing clover, 'Stealing Turnips poaching and breaking into Hen Roosts and Things of that Kind', and thieving clothes, game birds, fish, sheep and vegetables. They were suspected of milking cows secretly at night. Pilfering cargoes was a constant year-round temptation. Always on the move, never stopping long, boat families, like gypsies, were a handy social group to blame for local mischief.

Down from the Midlands came the slow boats, up from the Fens, along the rivers and canals which fed into the Humber or into the Thames, where the great pull of London was strong: a steady procession of boats and barges under sail or towed by old ponies, Shires, Spanish mules or pairs of donkeys urged onwards by women and stumbling children. A small boy sitting on a quietly waiting horse...a heavy-loaded barge...rustic-looking lock gates...a Suffolk meadow — this was the world which Constable, in a series of heroic paintings of life on the Stour, saw, observed, and understood. Those great pastoral anthems recorded scenes on a rural river navigation in the 1820s. In towns the story was different.

On the Regent's Canal in the 1880s the journalist Ellis Martin heard tales of ruffians and loitering boys 'wot calls yer names and spits on yer and throws stones at yer — nothin' else. Then, if yer complains they pelts yer with brickbats wuss'n ever...'. Bill Gibbins, recalling life on his parents' narrow boats in the 1920s, recalled that in the Black Country the 'water was like ink because it was going in and out of the factories all the time'. He remembered starting the working day at 'about 4 or 5 o'clock' and travelling a long way before a cup of tea and breakfast. Someone had to lead the horses all the way, or else they stopped to eat from the hedgerow or the greensward. 'You walked a lot of miles', recalled Bill Gibbins. A 12 to 15 hour day and a 7-day week was quite normal on the cut, even in the final mid-twentieth century period. It could take a good day's work, say 18 hours, to run a pair of loaded boats (a motor boat towing an unpowered butty) between Birmingham and Braunston. On top of this, boatmen were usually expected to load and unload their own cargoes. Payment was per ton of cargo delivered. Despite the long hours, a boatman's earning power was not great.

On the cut, boundaries between working and socializing blurred. Boatmen created their own habits and rituals to break up the arduous journeys. They looked out for simple things: boats run by relatives, a favourite water-tap, a hedge full of wild plums, a canalside shop. Keeping up a steady pace ($2\frac{1}{2}$ miles an hour or so if horse-towed) they tried to be first through the locks. And looking out from the narrow line which they travelled they caught glimpses of other canal or industry-related territory: labourers harvesting in the fields; dusty carts (and later lorries) heading towards coalyards; gesticulating lock-keepers; factory clerks chalking up boat arrivals; a goods train suddenly erupting across a bridge. At night when the going had been good, a visit to the pub was not uncommon. There the talk was familiar, often coarse, and full of the reflected life of the cut — of boats and cargoes, stoppages, hold-ups, punch-ups, births, marriages, deaths and journeys' ends. The boatmen's lingo was a pungent mix of swearing and strange jargon, peppered with a Great War kind of slang. There was an almost superstitious reluctance to call things by their proper names. Everything was called something else. The Shropshire Union was the 'Sloppy Cut', Marsworth was 'Maffers', Birmingham was 'Brumagem' or 'Birnigum', Atherstone became 'Ariston', Walsall was 'the Ganzees'. Flights of locks were known as 'thicks'. Boats and their parts often had odd names. There were 'reso's and 'odd'ns' on the Basingstoke Canal, and 'toe rags' on the Worcester and Birmingham. A boat's rudder was called the 'ellum'. 'Ole' was a useful word — as in 'ingin' 'ole' (engine hold) 'bridge

'ole' (the space beneath the arch of a bridge) and 'Jam 'ole Run' (the Grand Union coal run to the Southall jam factory). Boatmen on the Oxford south of Napton were known as 'Bread and Larders' while those who worked F.M.C. boats were 'Greasy Ockers'. 'Going ashore' meant stepping off the boat. To 'Bell Oil' something meant to hit it hard.

George Smith identified sensational drunkenness and violence as two of the facts of Victorian canal life. More common risks were being kicked by a horse or crushed by a boat or cargo. The greatest danger was the water itself. Night journeys, especially in winter, were hazardous. In pitch-black darkness the feeble glimmer of an oil-lamp and the faded white ends of lock beams were little help to a tired boat family. Death by drowning was not infrequent. At the canal village of Stoke Bruerne, parish registers covering the period 1830 to 1900 record many tragedies, often involving drowned children: John Hall, aged 1 year 11 months; Joseph Scaldwell, $6\frac{1}{2}$; Frederick Jeffery, aged 3; 'a person unknown, aged about 13'; an unidentified woman 'drowned in a lock of the canal'.

In the 1870s decent middle-class people were horrified to learn that England possessed a 'floating' population of over 100,000 people who were living 'in a state of wretchedness, misery, immorality, cruelty, and evil training'. George Smith was exaggerating both the figures and probably the misery, although by the 1870s railway competition was pressing hard on many canal companies, keeping wages low and conditions unimproved. Sunday (as well as all-night) working was now common. The canal population and its ways had been 'discovered' by society and Smith's emotive campaign compelled action on behalf of the boatmen. Action came in the form of the Canal Boats Acts and in the setting up of various Christian schools and missions; though these were not the first attempts at providing for the educational and spiritual welfare of the boatmen.

108 *The Church takes them under its wing: the Bishop of Bermuda dedicates the Grand Union's floating school barge 'Elsdale' in 1930 (BW Archives).*

Chapels, churches and missions (108)

Canal ports, especially the new settlements where there were no established churches, attracted nonconformist ministries from early on. The Methodist chapel at Stourport was built in the 1780s and enlarged in 1812. Runcorn, apparently, needed especial ministry. A Welsh chapel was built there in 1807. In 1818 the Huntingtonians arrived, in 1829 the Welsh Calvinists and Congregationalists, in 1835 the Independents, in 1838 the Primitives, in 1846 the Baptists and newly emancipated Roman Catholics. The Church of England built a new church in 1838 and another by the architect Salvin in 1847–9. Finally two Methodist chapels were built in the 1860s and 1870s. All these places of worship were not built solely for the canal boatmen, but the local population included many who worked on boats or at the docks. For those reluctant or unable to step far from the water, there was a mariners' chapel in Old Quay Docks and a floating chapel on the Bridgewater Canal. Floating chapels were a cheap and cheerful way of reaching the boatmen on their own terms. There was one moored near Hythe Bridge in Oxford in the early years of the twentieth century; a less exuberant version of the college barges which adorned the Isis.

The religious revival movements of the 1840s created an atmosphere in which the provision of churches was seen as highly desirable. In

109 *Gritty, soot-darkened Gothic: Christ Church, Weston Point Docks. Built in 1841 by the Weaver Navigation Trustees, who took the spiritual needs of boatmen seriously* (BW Archives).

1840, the little Christ Church was built next to the branch canal at Glasson Dock and in 1843–48 the Aire & Calder Company belatedly built the church of St John at Goole. This large church was designed by William Hurst and W. B. Moffat in a workmanlike Gothic Revival style. It still thrusts boldly into the dock area, its spire adding a sharp touch to the skyline of hoists, cranes and jumbled warehouse roofs. Christ Church at Weston Point (**109**) has an even more forcible presence. It was built in 1841, right in the heart of the docks. There was no mistaking who were the expected congregation of this church built by the trustees of the Weaver Navigation. Two others were built by the same trustees: Holy Trinity in Northwich in 1842 and Christ Church in Winsford in 1844. When the Winsford church subsided and had to be demolished, it was replaced by another, timber-framed one in 1882. These churches were built for use by boatmen and other staff.

The trustees paid for ministers and choirs and provided hymn books. Few companies were as conscientious as this: in Stourport the Staffs & Worcester Canal Company only managed to rent a pew in a local church.

Gloucester Docks has a Mariners' Chapel (**110**) fitted out in a sparse, nautical way, its stone walls and clear-cut lines adding dignity and contrast to the great brick warehouses massed around it. Worshippers at Sharpness New Dock made do with a prefabricated, corrugated-iron church, similar to many Church of England missions built from the 1880s onwards in newly populated industrial areas. Occasionally there were chapels at smaller wharfs and basins. There was a cheese warehouse-cum-chapel at Nantwich. At Tyrley Wharf, services were sometimes held in the community room which formed part of the neat lockside development. Some canal boatmen sought God in their own way, perhaps like Thomas Smallwood, a Roman Catholic lock-keeper who in the early nineteenth century practised his faith quietly in Middle Lock Cottage at Hillmorton.

In the mid nineteenth century, societies and missions became increasingly active in targeting boatmen. Among others there were the Boatmen's Pastoral Instruction Society, the Boatmen's Friend Society and the Paddington Society for Promoting Christian Knowledge among Canal Boatmen and Others. This society had its own chapel and shops, and published a canal boatmen's magazine which ran for a few years in the 1830s. Mission rooms and institutes were built in towns and dock areas. There were several mission buildings (coyly referred to as 'coffee rooms') on the BCN. One at Tipton originally had a wooden belfry. The Boatmen's Rest, built in 1900 at Walsall Top Lock, has Venetian Gothic windows and is now a museum. There were other missions in Sheffield, York, Goole and Ellesmere Port. A mission in Leeds had stables, a kitchen, a wash-house and a (non-alcoholic) refreshment room. A later, fussily domestic 'Boatmen's Institute'

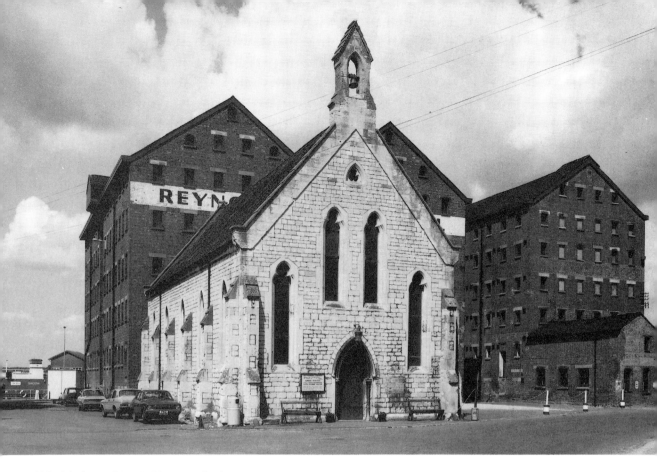

110 *Mariners' Chapel, Gloucester Docks; spare architectural details with a simple, ship-shape interior* (RCHME Crown Copyright).

(**111**) survives at Brentford, dated 1904. The Salvation Army provided an unrivalled service, working from wharfs or boats where they could literally 'get alongside' the boat families.

The people who ran the canal missions were usually real Christians who wanted to try and help. Other do-gooders and 'preachers' were spurred on by George Smith's proclamations of the boatman's illiteracy, his squalor and his abuse of women and children by making them work hard. Smith and others like him had gone out and done their research on some of the filthiest canals in England. Part of the problem was that the canals were in decline. The other point is that Smith singled out canals because he had a personal interest in them. Conditions for many of the Victorian working class were just as appalling.

111 *Boatmen's Institute, Brentford: A fussy, domestic-looking building where the London City Mission provided a reading room, laundry, soft drinks and 'counselling'* (BW Archives).

112 *Hard at work aboard 'Elsdale', the floating classroom moored at Bull's Bridge in the 1930s (*BW Archives*).*

Schools

One of the most noticeable things about a canal boatman was his lack of education. 'They are extremely illiterate, uninstructed and depraved', Sir George Chetwynd told a select committee in 1841. For many boat children there were few chances of regularly attending school.

The Weaver Navigation provided several schools along with its churches. These served a fairly static population, as did those built at docks. By 1837 Goole had six schools. Following the extension of the Lancaster Canal a school was built at Glasson Dock. In the 1870s a Gothic Revival school was built in a bracing corner of Sharpness New Dock. Missions opened schools when they could afford to do so. There was a London City Mission school at

Brentford in the 1890s. Floating schools, like floating chapels, were another attempt at bringing the 'three Rs' to the canalside. The Grand Union Canal Co. provided one at Bull's Bridge in the 1930s (**112**).

Although the 1884 Canal Boats Act required local authorities to ensure that boat children attended school, enforcement of the law was sporadic and difficult. In Birmingham boat children went to local schools when they could, and in theory this happened elsewhere too. But discrimination by other children and sometimes teachers was not uncommon. Harry Fletcher helped his father run a Humber keel between Hull and Sheffield in the early twentieth century and recalled that he 'seldom went to school' although he once attended for three weeks 'at Keadby while we were waiting for a cargo of coal'. The local schools were rough and the children ganged up on the 'keely dogs'.

In the end, Harry Fletcher reckoned he 'got no more than six months' of education in his whole life (**113**).

It is not possible now to re-create or even wholly explain the world of England's working boatmen. Men and boats, men and horses: these images are as old as history. But only in England does there emerge, for a short time, an extraordinary pattern of building, trading and living on a dense network of industrial canals. Living and working on boats far inland, boats which often travelled long distances and were pulled, to begin with, by horses, was a unique experience. It had a connectedness about it which was generated by its context; by the obvious routes, the functional buildings and boats, the visual forms and monochrome colours of canal paraphernalia. These artificial things informed and organized the boatman's

experience. They were his terms of reference, to which he brought his own working methods, habits of life, values and stories. Life on the cut was a world of overlapping and contrasting relationships: cargoes and journeys, loading and unloading, stables and pubs, boats and docks, aqueducts and tunnels, water and land, sunlit countryside and 'six counties overhung with smoke'. Between the 1760s when it began and the 1960s when it ended, generations of boatmen and their families were born, grew up, and died in a narrow world that might be 100 miles long but only 50 feet wide. And despite spending their entire lives on boats and water, few of them ever saw the sea.

113 *A few simple lives, set apart and played out on a boat floating in a narrow world of water (*BW Archives*).*

Further reading

Anyone looking into waterways history must stand on Charles Hadfield's shoulders. His comprehensive series *The Canals of the British Isles* provides deep insights into the past fortunes of canal companies. The series includes an introductory volume, *British Canals* (1969 and later editions) and the following detailed studies; *The Canals of the East Midlands* (1970), *The Canals of South and South East England* (1969), *The Canals of South Wales and the Border* (1967), *The Canals of South West England* (1967), *The Canals of the West Midlands* (1967), *The Canals of Yorkshire and North East England* (2 vols; 1972–73) and by C. Hadfield and G. Biddle, *The Canals of North West England* (2 vols; 1970). J. Boyes and R. Russell, *The Canals of Eastern England* (1977) is a later addition to the series. A compendious, wide-ranging reference work covering most aspects of Britain's waterways is E. W. Paget-Tomlinson, *The Complete Book of Canal and River Navigation* (1993). L.T.C. Rolt, *Navigable Waterways*, (revised edition, 1985) is a good general introduction, as is C. Hadfield, *The Canal Age* (1968). E. de Maré, *The Canals of England* (reprinted 1988) is full of evocative photographs. The best history of early waterways is still T. S. Willan, *River Navigation in England 1600–1750* (1936). R. Russell, *Lost Canals of England and Wales* (1982) is a guide to abandoned waterways.

Books dealing with more specific architectural/engineering topics include H. Conway-Jones, *Gloucester Docks* (1984); J. D. Porteous, *Canal Ports* (1978); D.H. Tew, *Canal Lifts and Inclined Planes (1985)*. Waterways craft are covered by E.W. Paget-Tomlinson, *Britain's Canal & River Craft* (1979); T. Chaplin, *Narrow Boats* (1989) and A. J. Lewery, *Narrow Boat Painting* (1974). The world of the working boatman is explored by H. Hanson, *The Canal Boatmen 1760–1914* (1975).

There are many publications covering individual waterways, from in-depth studies like I. Langford, *The Staffordshire and Worcestershire Canal* (1974); M. Clarke, *The Leeds and Liverpool Canal* (1990); K.R. Clew, *The Kennet & Avon Canal* (reprinted 1985); A.H. Faulkner, *The Grand Junction Canal* (1993) and P. Smith, *The Aire & Calder Navigation* (1987), to smaller but no less interesting booklets like J. Morris, *The Shropshire Union Canal* (1991), the Old Union Canals Society, *The 'Old Union' Canals* (1990) and D. Goodwin, *Foxton Locks and the Grand Junction Canal Co.* (1988). Probably the best archaeology-based study of any canal is S. Hughes, *The Archaeology of the Montgomeryshire Canal* (3rd edition 1988).

Biographies of engineers range from A.W. Skempton, *The Engineers of the English River Navigations, 1620–1760* (Trans. Newcomen Society 29. 1953) to C.T. Boucher, *James Brindley* (1970) and *John Rennie* (1963) L.T.C. Rolt, *Thomas Telford* (1958) and C. Hadfield and A.W. Skempton, *William Jessop, Engineer* (1979). C. Hadfield, *Thomas Telford's Temptation* (1993) is a recent re-appraisal.

Original sources, several of which are available as reprints, include J.A. Phillips, *General History of Inland Navigation Foreign and Domestic* (1792); R. Fulton, *Treatise on the Improvement of Canal Navigation* (1796); an essay, written by John Farey, on 'Canals' in A. Rees *Cyclopaedia* (1819); J. Priestley, *Historical Account of the Navigable Rivers, Canals and Railways throughout Great Britain* (1831); T. Telford, *Life of Thomas Telford* (1838). A different note is struck by G. Smith, *Our Canal Population* (reprinted 1975).

Vivid accounts of waterway life are found in E.T. Thurston, *The Flower of Gloster* (reprinted 1985); Harry Fletcher, *A Life on the Humber* (1975) and L.T.C. Rolt, *Narrow Boat* (1944).

There are many guides, booklets and leaflets produced by canal societies and local history societies. The monthly magazine *Waterways World* (1972 onwards) covers canal history, boats and past and present events on Britain's waterways.

Gazetteer

There are numerous waterways in the British Isles. Many are still in use or are undergoing restoration. Others are disused, overgrown or barely traceable on the ground. This gazetteer lists those canals and river navigations which offer reasonable access and substantial remains. Selection has been made with both chronology and geography in mind. There are early river navigations and late canals here, from places as far apart as Cornwall, Cumbria, and Essex. The gazetteer gives no more than a snapshot of each waterway; the main date of its opening, the names of its engineers, and something of its flavour and features. Most of what is here is either visible or easily approached by boat or on foot. Not all waterway sites are freely open to the public, and caution is urged upon those who set out to explore lost or abandoned canals.

Aire & Calder Navigation (1702 John Hadley) A big, commercial waterway. Now dotted with silent sites of former industry. Revitalised Leeds warehouse quarter. Stanley Ferry Aqueduct. Mechanised locks with control cabins and coloured light signals. Port of Goole.

Ashby Canal (1804 Robert Whitworth, Thomas Newbold) A sleepy contour canal which ends quietly in a field. A handful of stone bridges, and Snarestone Tunnel, which runs beneath a village.

Ashton Canal (c1796) An unglamorous urban canal; not as grim as it used to be. Sturdy aqueducts, locks, and patchwork bridges. Warehouses reclaimed for other uses. Group of buildings at Fairfield Junction includes toll office, canal agent's house and packet boat house of 1833.

Basingstoke Canal (1794 William Jessop) Southern canal with beautiful stretches and a 20-mile (32km) summit. Greywell Tunnel built in the 1790s. Undergoing restoration.

Birmingham Canal Navigations (1770s onwards: various engineers) The hub of England's waterways; a complicated multi-level maze of Pioneering, Heroic and Late canals. Main canals include: Birmingham Canal (Old Main Line 1772, New Main Line 1838), Birmingham & Fazeley Canal (1789), Wyrley & Essington (c. 1795), Dudley Canal (lines in 1779, 1792, 1798), Tame Valley Canal (1844). Overlapping scenery: dishevelled and seedy to 'tidied up'; poignantly decayed to recently re-developed. Full of strong visual impressions: majestic New Main Line slicing through grimy guts of Birmingham; open and closed views; factory-lined dead-ends, loops and deserted basins; empty toll islands; swooping iron bridges; boatmens' toilets slotted into brick walls; big Victorian engineering and primitive but long-lasting Georgian remains. Highlights include: Gas Street Basin (water-filled spaces, boats, a handful of cottages and warehouses), Farmer's Bridge Locks, Smethwick Cutting and Galton Bridge, Netherton Tunnel, Rotton Park Reservoir, Delph Locks, Wolverhampton Locks, Sheepcote Street stables, the Boatmen's Rest at Walsall Top Lock. The Black Country

Museum features canal exhibits, Dudley Tunnel, and a working BCN boatyard. For grandeur and grimness combined the Tame Valley Canal should be seen. Stourbridge Canal (1779) links BCN with Staffs & Worcester Canal and has fine Bonded Warehouse at Stourbridge, and sixteen-lock flight at Wordsley.

Bridgewater Canal (1761 Duke of Bridgewater, John Gilbert, James Brindley) Historic, large-scale Pioneering canal. Big embankments. Prototype standard design bridges. Packet Boat House and canal entrance to mines at Worsley Delph. Barton swing-aqueduct. Forlorn canal-side warehouses culminating in partly restored Castlefield Basin area.

Bridgwater & Taunton Canal (1827 James Hollinsworth) Isolated, slightly eerie canal. Locks with counterweighted gearing. Walled cutting and hand-worked dock in Bridgwater deserve to be better known.

Bude Canal (1823 James Green) Rare example of a 'manure canal', with a sea-lock at Bude Harbour. Scattered remnants of small warehouses and large inclined planes.

Calder & Hebble Navigation (1770 John Smeaton, James Brindley) Mid eighteenth century (and later) with Pennine horizons. Stone locks, cottages and warehouses, especially at Sowerby Basin. One splendid warehouse, in Wakefield.

Caldon Canal (c. 1779) Secretive branch of Trent & Mersey. Remains of canalside industry and unexpected visual beauty in 'lost valley' setting of Cheddleton. Interesting infrastructure, especially at Denford where Leek Branch runs alongside and crosses main line on aqueduct near Hazelhurst Locks; a complete 'canalscape' of the 1840s.

Caledonian Canal (1822 Thomas Telford) Coast-to-coast ship canal linking Loch Ness and others in spectacular setting as at Fort Augustus, Corpach, Inverness. Big cuttings and big locks, including 'Neptune's Staircase' at Banavie. Similar to Sweden's Gotha Canal, also designed by Telford.

River Cam (Always navigable; improved after 1702 Act) Roman navigation, improved over centuries. Originally linked by navigable lodes to large villages. Jesus Lock in Cambridge has bay-fronted cottage, lock with swan-neck beams, swing footway and iron footbridge. Commissioners' Banqueting House at Horningsea.

Chelmer & Blackwater Navigation (1797 John Rennie) Shallow eastern waterway, unkempt and largely rural. Basin and 'warehouse-as-temple' at Heybridge. Sail-lofts, maltings, and Essex character in small port of Maldon.

Chesterfield Canal (1777 James Brindley, Hugh Henshall, John Varley) Extensive staircases. Fine straddle warehouse in Worksop. Half-buried locks and frighteningly small tunnel at Norwood on disused stretch.

Coventry Canal (1790 James Brindley, Edmund Lingard, Samuel Bull) Chequered history and interesting remains: Coventry Basin, Hawkesbury Junction, Hartshill Yard. Bridges of many shapes and dates. Interplay of town and country. Faint flavour of decay.

Crinan Canal (1801 John Rennie) Ship canal cut through difficult Argyll terrain. Nine miles (14.5km), 15 locks. Hand-operated roller or draw-back bridge at Dunardry; intimate basin at Crinan.

Cromford Canal (1794 William Jessop, Benjamin Outram) Derbyshire drama and extensive engineering: broad locks, narrow tunnels and stone aqueducts. Important sites at Cromford, close to Arkwright's first cotton factory, and Leawood Pumping Station. Canal-related tramroad from Cromford Wharf to Whaley Bridge.

Driffield Navigation (1770) Humber keel navigation. Good group of buildings including warehouse, granaries, mill, cranes, at head of navigation in dusty town of Gt Driffield.

Exeter Canal (1566 John Trew; 1830 James Green) Cut by Elizabethans but much altered. Characterful nineteenth-century warehouses in Exeter Basin. Turf Hotel, at Turf Lock, designed by engineer James Green.

Forth & Clyde Canal (1790 John Smeaton, Robert Whitworth) Britain's oldest and longest coast-to-coast ship canal, graced by a series of architecturally effective structures: twin-leaved lift (or bascule) bridges, classical offices and stable blocks, Kelvin Aqueduct. Undergoing restoration.

Fossdyke & Witham Navigations (Fossdyke has Roman origins; Witham always navigable) Eastern waterways in a flat, remote land. Sparse features include: Torksey Lock, Brayford Pool in Lincoln, and the Grand Sluice in Boston. Boston, once a great river port, with part-restored, part-decayed warehouses.

Gloucester & Sharpness Canal (1827 Robert Mylne) Bleak, windswept ship canal. Sharpness Docks at one end; Gloucester Docks (National Waterways Museum) at the other. Greek Revival bridge-keepers' houses in between.

Grand Union Canal 1929 union of older, separate waterways linking London and Birmingham. These included: Warwick & Birmingham Canal (1799) Grand Junction Canal (1805 William Jessop), Warwick & Napton Canal (1800), Regent's Canal (1820) q.v. Trunk canal with long main line. Much of interest: complete 1930s canalscapes, e.g. at Knowle and Hatton, with locks, bridges, stables, plank sheds, pump-houses, and cottages. Earlier pumping stations and cottages further south. Braunston and Blisworth Tunnels. Settlements at Braunston and Stoke Bruerne. Victorian Bulbourne Yard. Big embankments and Tring Cutting engineered by Jessop. Multi-locked arm to Northampton. Arms to Slough, Wendover and Aylesbury. Leicester Line (formerly the old Grand Union 1814) includes Foxton and Watford Locks and rural summit.

Grand Western Canal (1814 John Rennie, John Thomas) Disused, with scattered archaeological remains. Bridges at Halberton, Sampford Peverel, Westleigh. Aqueducts at Halberton and Nynehead Court. Lime kilns and wharf at Tiverton.

Huddersfield Narrow Canal (1811 Benjamin Outram) Narrow-gauge trans-Pennine route. Highest canal, with longest tunnel (Standedge) in England. Water supplied by 10 moorland reservoirs. Stone cottages and warehouse at Marsden. Converted, late eighteenth-century stone-built warehouse at Huddersfield.

Kennet & Avon Canal (Kennet 1724, Avon 1727 both John Hore; Canal 1810 John Rennie) Nineteenth-century east-west canal linking (and now including) two eighteenth-century river navigations. Bold architectural gestures at western end (especially in Bath) stone aqueducts, fine bridges, wooden swing-bridges, Caen Hill flight of locks. Pumping stations of great interest at Claverton and Crofton. At eastern end stands Garston Lock, the last turf-sided lock in England.

Lancaster Canal (1819 John Rennie, Thomas Fletcher, William Crosley) Isolated canal with mixed scenery. Fine collection of curvy, well-modelled stone bridges and minor aqueducts. Lune Aqueduct. Glasson Dock sea outlet on 1825 branch with impressive locks. Disused northern stretches are splendid: theatrical architecture — Sedgwick Aqueduct, Hincaster Tunnel — with back-cloth of Cumbrian hills.

Lee (or Lea) and Stort Navigations (Lee always navigable; Stort 1769 Thomas Yeoman) London-orientated malt and timber waterways. Ancient River Lee has altered locks, dour brown brick cottages and great, hump-backed sheds at Ferry Lane Wharf, Tottenham. Tributary Stort a pretty, winding river with occasional cottages and a dead-end in Bishop's Stortford.

Leeds & Liverpool Canal (1816 John Longbotham, Robert Whitworth, Samuel Fletcher) Broad trans-Pennine canal. $127\frac{1}{4}$ miles (205km) long with 91 (later 92) locks. Plenty of eye-catching structures and details: solid-looking sandstone bridges and locks; Bingley Five Rise Locks, Foulridge Tunnel, canal settlement with yard, dry dock, cottages at Burscough. Extraordinary Burnley embankment typifies scale and ambitions of this canal. Great shuttered warehouses (home to cats and starlings) slowly coming back to life in Burnley, Blackburn, Wigan, Leeds.

Llangollen Canal (formerly Ellesmere Canal, 1805 William Jessop, Thomas Telford) Mania canal with outstanding engineering: Chirk Aqueduct and Tunnel, Pontcysyllte Aqueduct and approach embankments, Horseshoe Falls feeder weir, lock staircase and cottage at Grindley Brook. Rare, surviving wooden lift bridges (two on Prees Branch). Welsh stretches are hilly and picturesque in the eighteenth century sense.

Louth Canal (1770 John Grundy) Canalisation of River Lud, which once took masted ships. Now disused. Early, scallop-sided lock at Alvingham. Basin and warehouses in Louth recall Driffield Navigation.

Macclesfield Canal (1831 William Crosley the younger) Confidently engineered late Heroic canal, built of crisply cut stone. Superb bridges (especially turnovers) aqueducts, and Bosley Locks.

Manchester Ship Canal (1894 E. Leader Williams) High Victorian engineering in the spirit which built the railways. Massive locks and swing-bridges, stark stretches of water, vanished docks.

Middle Level Navigations Fenland system of drains/navigations linking rivers Ouse and Nene. Owes much to work of Vermuyden, completed 1651. Huge sky-scenery and flat landscape bisected by embanked waterways where boats often ride above farms and fields. Empty miles of water with scattered engineering: sluices, pointing doors, occasional locks in strange, remote places.

Monmouthshire & Brecon Canal (formerly Monmouthshire Canal 1799 Thomas Dadford the younger and Brecknock & Abergavenny Canal 1812 Thomas Dadford the younger, Thomas Cartwright, William Crosley) Isolated Welsh waterway in National Park. Built high up along hillsides, with many tramroad connections to ironworks. Four-arched Brynich

Aqueduct, Ashford Tunnel and white, toy-like toll house at Pontymoile. Plenty of coarse-textured stone bridges in idyllic green scenery. Impressive flight of fourteen locks at Rogerstone on the Crumlin branch.

Montgomery Canal (1797 John Dadford, Thomas Dadford the elder and the younger. Western branch 1821 John Williams) Quiet agricultural canal with outstanding scenery. Interesting equipment and remains of various dates incuding aqueducts, locks, bridges and wharfs. Undergoing restoration.

Neath Canal (1795 Thomas Dadford the younger, Thomas Sheasby the elder) Archetypal South Wales canal which served a coalfield valley. Part-restored. Excellent eleven arched aqueduct on short Tennant Canal (1829) which joined it at Aberdulais.

River Ouse (Yorkshire. Always navigable up to York; improved in eighteenth and nineteenth centuries) Links with Ure Navigation and Ripon Canal. Banqueting House, big locks, weir, swing-bridges and ancillary buildings at Naburn. York riverfront is lined with re-developed industrial/commercial sites.

Oxford Canal (1790 James Brindley, Samuel Simcock; 1834 William Cubitt) Supreme early contour canal later straightened and modernised. Links with Thames at Oxford. Lush southern stretches running in and out of River Cherwell; harsher, brickier northern stretches. Lonely summit with wooden lift-bridges. Hump-backed bridges of limestone or brick. Scattered locks, some with cottages. Tooley's Yard in Banbury, Hillmorton Yard near Rugby.

Peak Forest Canal (1804 Benjamin Outram) Fine stone engineering especially Marple Locks and Marple Aqueduct. Whaley Bridge (rail/canal transhipment shed) and Bugsworth Basin (canal/tramway transhipment centre) are important archaeological sites. Bugsworth includes remains of a gauging lock, basins and wharfs, tramways and battery of lime kilns.

Pocklington Canal (1818 George Leather) Lonely canal bounded by water-meadows. Re-used canal warehouse at canal head. Strange and rare bridges at Hagg, Walbut and Coates. Undergoing restoration.

Regent's Canal (1820 James Morgan) London canal hemmed by parks and buildings ranging from Little Venice's posh villas to Grimshaw's space-age terrace and the tower blocks and fly-blown wharfs of Hackney. Iron bridges on Zoo stretch and Macclesfield Bridge, Islington Tunnel, Camden Lock, St Pancras Lock. Ends in re-developed Regent's Canal Dock (Limehouse Basin).

Rochdale Canal (1804 William Jessop, John Rennie, William Crosley the elder) First broad trans-Pennine canal. Still run by Rochdale Canal Co. Big stone warehouses in Manchester and at Sowerby Bridge junction with Calder & Hebble. March Barn Bridge a good skew example.

River Severn (Always navigable; nineteenth-century improvements) Big dangerous river. Naturally navigable to Pool Quay near Welshpool until late nineteenth century. Big locks and weirs of 1840s at Lincomb, Holt, Bevere, Diglis. Links Gloucester Docks, Stourport and the Ironbridge Gorge.

Sheffield & South Yorkshire Navigation Modern system of older canals including short Don Navigation, Dearne & Dove Canal (1804). Sheffield Canal (1819) with basin and warehouses at Sheffield; wide and flat Stainforth & Keadby (*c.* 1802) and Late phase, straight New Junction Canal (1905); England's last manmade waterway.

Shrewsbury Canal (1796 Josiah Clowes; Thomas Telford) Disused tub-boat canal: remains include earliest iron aqueduct at Longdon-on-Tern, straddle warehouse and bridge at Wappenshall, ruined guillotine locks, Greek Revival warehouse in Shrewsbury.

Shropshire Canal (1792 William Reynolds) Hill-climbing tub-boat canal now disused. Main remains are restored Hay inclined plane and Coalport Wharf at Ironbridge Gorge Museum complex.

Shropshire Union Canal Union of older canals including Ellesmere Canal Wirral Line (1797) and Chester Canal (1779) with impressive Chester stretch. Main part is former Birmingham & Liverpool Junction (1835) revealing the hand and mind of Telford. Junction with Shrewsbury Canal at Norbury. Deep cuttings like Tyrley, big embankments as at Shelmore, iron aqueducts like that at Nantwich, stone bridges, straight lines; standardisation but no staleness. The *ne plus ultra* of the Canal Age.

Staffordshire & Worcestershire Canal (1772 James Brindley, Samuel Simcock, Thomas Dadford the elder) Colloquially always the 'Staffs & Worcester'. Easy-going eighteenth-century canal with Stourport as its terminus. Pioneering aqueducts, bridges and locks with curiously shaped by-weirs. Staircase at Bratch Locks. Sole remaining round-house at Gailey Wharf.

Stratford-on-Avon Canal (Northern section 1796 Josiah Clowes; southern section 1816 William Whitmore) Earlier, duller northern section: guillotine lock and tunnel at King's Norton, Brandwood Tunnel with Shakespeare medallion plaque. Charming, incidental southern section: three cast-iron trough aqueducts (Edstone is England's second longest) barrel-roofed cottages, mouldering split-bridges.

Tavistock Canal (1817 John Taylor) Short, disused copper-carrying canal. Group of stone-built cottages and warehouses at Tavistock Wharf.

River Thames (Always navigable) Ancient water highway with its own character, atmosphere and style. Course through London followed by 135 tideless meandering miles from Teddington to Cricklade via medieval river ports of Henley, Abingdon, Oxford. The towpath is a relic of commercial days. Charming lock cottages range in date from eighteenth to twentieth centuries. House colours of white, grey, black, on lock gates, weirs, footbridges; following nautical traditions. Still has uniformed lock-keepers.

Thames & Severn Canal (1789 Josiah Clowes) Legendary, problematic canal built for sailing barges. Expressively handled Cotswold stone architecture of circular watch houses, wharf houses and two faces of Sapperton Tunnel. Undergoing restoration.

River Trent (Part always navigable. Improvements from 1770s onwards) Big, commercial waterway, lined with batteries of re-used and decaying warehousing and maltings at places like Gainsborough and Newark, including rare mass-concrete structures.

Trent & Mersey Canal (1777 James Brindley, Hugh Henshall) Pioneering trunk canal, with lingering eighteenth-century style, especially in bridges. Shardlow a small canal town. Fradley Yard and Junction with good group of buildings. Harecastle Old and New tunnels stand side by side. Scenery varies from bucolic pasture to urban potteries.

Ulverston Canal (1796 John Rennie) Short, wide, Cumbrian ship canal which turned Ulverston into a port. Terminates in basin with curving Sunderland Terrace (canal-related housing) on western side.

Weaver Navigation (1732 Thomas Robinson; 1897 E. Leader Williams) Eighteenth-century navigation largely rebuilt in Late Victorian era. Grand, underrated waterway. Big locks, (with 'Aztec' stonework and semaphore signals) big sluices, big swing-bridges, Anderton boat lift which transferred boats between Weaver and Trent & Mersey Canal.

Wey Navigation (1653 Sir Richard Weston & son) Rare example of southern river navigation begun in 1650s. Locks originally turf-sided. Links with Basingstoke Canal.

Worcester & Birmingham Canal (1815 Thomas Cartwright, John Woodhouse, William Crosley the younger) Heroic narrow canal with many locks, tunnels and reservoirs. Lock-flight at Tardebigge is longest in Britain. Tardebigge Tunnel largely cut through solid rock. Wharf and maintenance yard nearby.

Index